This is a clear, down to earth and readable historical justification for having faith in the Jesus of history. It is up to date with the latest scholarship but doesn't blind the reader with unnecessary argument. I highly recommend it.

Alanna Nobbs, Professor Emerita
Department of Ancient History, Macquarie University, Sydney

Even a brief encounter with the written works or videos of John Dickson hints of his serious scholarship, willingness to engage the toughest critics of Christianity, and winsome ability to communicate. But *Is Jesus History?* is worth more than a cursory glance—you might even find yourself dog-earing page after page filled with archaeological gems and historical insight. This is a book you will want to pass on to both your skeptical and believing friends. But keep a copy for yourself.

Ravi Zacharias
Author and Speaker

With characteristic clarity and excellence of scholarship John Dickson examines the historical evidences for Jesus. His accessible style and bang-up-to-date sources make this a must read for anyone who is serious about investigating Jesus.

Dr Amy Orr-Ewing
Director, The Oxford Centre for Christian Apologetics

Is Jesus History? has a historian take us on a look at history as a discipline and compare what we know about Jesus with other ancient materials. It is a fascinating tour that also uncovers what ancient sources say about Jesus in the face of some who claim he never existed and we can know little about him. It is a tour well worth taking. It may well have you thinking very differently about events from long ago that still impact our world today.

Darrell Bock, Senior Research Professor
Dallas Theological Seminary, USA

Is Jesus History? is a provocative little book. John Dickson writes engagingly and personally—as you read, you can imagine having a coffee (or a pint) with him and laughing over the idiosyncrasies of the field of biblical studies, even while appreciating the hard work scholars do. Indeed, this book reads with deep appreciation for scholars, and thus serves as a translation of the current state of conversations in the field that can complicate the average person's understanding of who Jesus of Nazareth might have been. His summaries of the various perplexing questions people have about Jesus are erudite and disarming, inviting people to reevaluate their assumptions and re-encounter the Jesus of history in the Jesus of the Bible.

Mariam J. Kovalishyn
Regent College, Vancouver

This is an eminently readable and relevant introduction that debunks many misconceptions about the gospel accounts of Jesus.

Dr David Wenham
Wycliffe Hall, Oxford

John Dickson combines top-notch scholarship with an accessible, conversational style as he explains the ancient evidence surrounding the historical Jesus. *Is Jesus History?* compares how we trust statements from our family, friends and news outlets with how we trust ancient testimonies of all sorts, including Aristotle's *The Art of Rhetoric*, Luke's Gospel, and Pliny the Younger's Letter 6 about the eruption of Mount Vesuvius. Dickson's even-handed approach towards the evidence invites readers to draw their own conclusions about the Jesus of history.

Dr Lynn Cohick
Provost and Dean, Denver Seminary

John Dickson is one of our most reliable guides today to the historical background of the life of Jesus. He blends the scholarship of an academic with the down-to-earth accessibility of the best of teachers. This book is full of insights; it may well surprise many to know how much the historical record actually shows us about the man who stands at the centre of the faith of over two billion people today.

Sam Allberry
Speaker and Author

Is Jesus History?

JOHN DICKSON

Is Jesus History?
© John Dickson, 2019.
Reprinted 2020.

Published by:
The Good Book Company in partnership with
The Oxford Centre for Christian Apologetics and
The Zacharias Institute

thegoodbook.com | www.thegoodbook.co.uk
thegoodbook.com.au | thegoodbook.co.nz | thegoodbook.co.in

John Dickson has asserted his right under the Copyright, Designs and Patents
Act 1988 to be identified as author of this work.

A CIP catalogue record for this book is available from the British Library.

Unless otherwise indicated, Scripture quotations are from The Holy Bible,
English Standard Version (ESV), copyright © 2001 by Crossway, a publishing
ministry of Good News Publishers. Used by permission. All rights reserved.

ISBN: 9781784983659 | Printed in India

Design by André Parker

Contents

Introduction: Christianity's unavoidable problem

Christianity has a problem.

Only one, you might ask?

Unlike other religions, Christianity gambles its plausibility on *supposed* historical events. Christians don't just say otherworldly things like, "God loves you", "We all need forgiveness", and "Heaven is open to all". None of that sort of thing is the least bit confirmable, or falsifiable. We may mock such spiritual claims, but we cannot disconfirm them with counterevidence.

But that's not really how Christians talk. Listen closely, and you'll often hear them say things like "Jesus lived in the Galilean village of Nazareth", or "He had a widespread reputation as a healer", or "He caused a scandal in the temple of Jerusalem around AD 30", or "He suffered execution under a Roman governor named Pontius Pilate", or even "His tomb outside the city wall was found empty a few days after his crucifixion, and his disciples saw him alive."

Statements like these are not completely immune from historical scrutiny. They touch times and places we know quite a bit about. They intersect with other figures (like Pilate) about whom we have reasonably good information. The alleged events all take place in a cultural and political melting pot—Roman Galilee and Judaea—for which we have thousands of archaeological remains and hundreds of thousands of words of ancient inscriptions and written records.

When people proclaim an intangible thing like "the universal love of God", they are safe from scrutiny. But as soon as they say that their guy was crucified by the fifth governor of Judaea, they are stepping onto public turf—and someone is bound to want to challenge the claim. And *challenge* they do!

ATTACKING THE CLAIMS

For a few years now some of the best-selling books have been full-scale attacks on Christian claims by the world's most brilliant atheists: Richard Dawkins, Christopher Hitchens, Michel Onfray, Lawrence Krauss, and so on. Hitchens, who sadly died a few years ago, speaks of the "highly questionable existence of Jesus" and the "huge amount of fabrication" in the stories written about him in the Gospels, the biographies of Jesus now found in the New Testament, the second part of the Christian Bible. He goes on:

> *Either the Gospels are in some sense literal truth, or the whole thing is essentially a fraud and perhaps an immoral one at that. Well, it can be stated with certainty, and on their own evidence, that the Gospels are most certainly not literal truth. That means that many of the "sayings" and teachings of Jesus are hearsay upon hearsay upon hearsay, which helps explain their garbled and contradictory nature.*[1]

---

1   Christopher Hitchens, *God is Not Great: How Religion Poisons Everything.* (Twelve, 2007), p 114-121.

It's very strong stuff, and many similar-sounding statements can be found throughout the popular atheist literature of the last decade or two. And it is such good writing—at least Hitchens' prose is fabulous—that it is easy to get swept up into thinking that these public naysayers must have a strong body of expert opinion behind them.

FALSE IMPRESSIONS

The impression these writers leave us with, whether intended or not, is that specialists in the field of history also talk of the "highly questionable existence of Jesus" or the "huge amount of fabrication" in the Gospels. But this impression is dramatically false. Anyone who dips into the academic literature about the figure of Jesus will quickly discover that trained scholars, regardless of their religious or irreligious conviction, reckon we know quite a bit about the influential teacher from Nazareth.

An entire industry of "double-checking" the claims about Jesus of Nazareth has developed over the last 250 years. The study of the "historical Jesus" is a vast secular discipline today, found in major universities all around the world, including the two with which I have been most closely associated—Macquarie University and Sydney University, in Australia.

While there are certainly plenty of active Christians involved in this sub-discipline of ancient history, there are also a great many half-Christians, ex-Christians and Jewish scholars (lots of Jewish scholars), as well as self-confessed agnostics and atheists. This makes it very difficult for anyone writing and working in this field to get away with publishing theology under the guise of history, or privileging the biblical documents over non-biblical ones, or pretending we can "prove" most of what the New Testament says about Jesus.

The process of peer review—where scholars publish their work in professional journals only after it has been double-checked by two or more independent (and anonymous) scholars of rank—might not be foolproof but it certainly filters out any works of propaganda. It also reduces the risk of fraudulent claims, and it keeps scholars constantly mindful of the *rules* of the history game.

VESTED INTERESTS

At the same time, outside the universities and on the street this topic is filled with such emotion and vested interests that some folks won't accept *any* claim that points even vaguely in the direction of the historicity of Jesus. The other day I posted on social media a famous statement about Jesus from the great Albert Einstein, and it triggered quite a reaction from my sceptical friends and followers.

The great physicist was interviewed in 1929 by the journalist George Viereck and, among many other things, he was asked about some religious matters. It is well known that Einstein despised "revealed religion" as infantile; he did not even like the idea of a personal God. His religious outlook was little more than a vague hunch that behind the laws of nature there must be some "infinitely superior spirit and reasoning power". Fair enough.

But the thing that annoyed my atheist friends was Einstein's admiration for the historical figure (yes, *historical* figure) found in the New Testament Gospels. Here's a portion of the interview:

> Viereck: *"To what extent are you influenced by Christianity?"*
> Einstein: *"As a child, I received instruction both in the Bible and in the Talmud. I am a Jew, but I am enthralled by the luminous figure of the Nazarene."*
> Viereck: *"You accept the historical existence of Jesus?"*
> Einstein: *"Unquestionably! No one can read the Gospels without feeling the actual presence of Jesus. His personality pulsates in every word. No myth is filled with such life. How different, for instance, is the impression which we receive from an account of legendary heroes of antiquity like Theseus. Theseus and other heroes of his type lack the authentic vitality of Jesus."* [2]

Einstein's admiration for Jesus and his confidence that Jesus was a historical figure offer a nice contrast to the more recent dogmatism of the best-selling atheists, which is perhaps why my sceptical social-media friends were so resistant to accepting that the great physicist could ever have stated such glowing words about the founder of Christianity.

I literally had folks suggesting Viereck's interview itself was a fraud, even though—as I pointed out—it was published in one of 20th-century America's most widely read magazines.

I had to dig it out of the archives and post screenshots of the relevant pages of the interview before some would believe that Einstein said such a thing. Even then, I'm not sure other folk would accept it. Such is the power of preference to shape what we believe! More about that problem later.

This book is partly a spirited defence of the whole subject of history, as well as being (hopefully) a fair-minded

---

2   "What Life Means to Einstein", *Saturday Evening Post*, October 26, 1929.

account of one particular historical life. I am asking, "Is Jesus History?" but also "Why and how does history as a discipline work?"

We will explore ancient writings as well as modern methods. We will examine the role of "faith" or "trust" in all academic endeavours, including science. And we will briefly outline *what* we can confidently say about historical figures like Emperor Tiberius, Pontius Pilate, the High Priest Caiaphas, and, of course, Jesus of Nazareth, all of whom overlapped for a brief period of their careers in the late 20s and early 30s of what we call the *first* century.

History and reality

For the last decade or so I have worn a silver *denarius* on a chain around my neck. This Roman coin was roughly equivalent to a day's wages in the first century—though it is worth a bit more today. Mine has the image of Emperor Tiberius on the front (the obverse) and his mother Livia on the back (the reverse). That tells us it was struck sometime between AD 14 and 37 (in the mint of Lyon, as it turns out), since the dates of Tiberius' reign are firmly established.

I wear this piece of Roman history partly for sentimental reasons. It is the coin Jesus of Nazareth famously pointed to—the denomination, not *the* very coin—when he was cornered over whether Jews in Judaea should pay taxes to Rome. "Whose image and inscription is this?," he asked as he indicated the *denarius*. "Caesar's," they all answered. "So give back to Caesar what is Caesar's," he responded, "and to God what is God's!" It is a very clever reply, with all sorts of fascinating implications about the separation of church and state. My ancient pendant has led to some fun conversations over the years, usually after someone asks me, "What's that around your neck? A Saint Christopher or something?"

A BRIDGE BACK IN TIME

But I also wear the coin for more intellectual reasons. It is a powerful reminder to me that the ancient past is as real and solid—or *was once* as real and solid—as this lump of metal around my neck.

I often take it in my fingers and let my imagination run wild. Perhaps a worker was handed this after a brutal twelve-hour shift in the ash mines of Naples. Maybe a senator tossed it to his musicians after a particularly pleasing performance of the "Song of Sicilus" (a hit in the day, with the key line "Enjoy life while you've got it"). What groceries did my coin buy? How many goblets of wine were drunk at its expense, in how many different cities? What sordid dealings did it pay for? Was it ever stolen? And who was the poor mug that eventually lost it in the dirt—from which it would be recovered almost twenty centuries later?

Our speculations could abound, of course, but my point is more substantial: the work, lives, loves, music, food, scandals and accidents of the first century were once just as real as the coin around my neck, and just as tangible as anything we smell, taste, touch, hear and see today.

My coin is a kind of bridge back in time. The inscriptions on it are vivid evidence of how Romans viewed their emperors: the Latin words around the edge read *divi Augusti filius*, son of the god Augustus (Tiberius' adoptive father).

The portraiture is semi-realistic: each emperor looks completely different, and they are mostly pretty ugly to our way of thinking. Google "Emperor Nero *denarius*", and you'll see what I mean. Tiberius put his mum on the back of his coins, idealised as the goddess *Pax* ("Peace"). That seems sweet, but it's complicated. He may have *owed* her, since rumours abounded that she had "removed" a couple of potential rivals. More concretely, her presence on such a widely-used coin underlines what ancient writings all affirm: this woman was a serious player in the politics of Rome, from the moment she divorced her first husband to marry Augustus in 39 BC through to her death in AD 29. These things we can say with a high degree of confidence.

History is real. It isn't Middle Earth or "a galaxy far, far away". It is part of the story of this same planet that we inhabit today. And all of us are biologically linked to people who lived in the same period (and perhaps the same place) that we are exploring in this book. Each of us has a great, great (x around 40) grandmother who lived, worked, hoped, ached, and laughed at the very time (late '20s of the first century) when Livia died, Tiberius ruled, Pontius Pilate harassed the residents of Judea, Jesus taught crowds in Galilee, and the prolific Roman author Pliny the Elder (AD 23-79) was starting primary school.

WHAT 1% OF EVIDENCE CAN TELL US

History is not just real; it is also *knowable*. Not *fully* knowable, of course. Probably less than 1% of ancient remains *remain* today. But 1% is enough to provide precious insight into the real lives of first-century men and women. Try this thought experiment...

Imagine people two thousand years from now digging up London and discovering 1% of the *Daily Mail*s, 1% of the city's statues and inscriptions, 1% of Marks & Spencer's receipts, 1% of the Parliamentary documents from Westminster, and 1% of the lost letters in the Royal Mail's National Returns Centre. While much of ordinary life from London 2019 would remain invisible to future historians, a great many other things could easily and reliably be known.

We would know the names of quite a few of the leaders of Great Britain, and around the world, too. We would know something of what people valued and memorialised. We would have some insight into the food people ate, how much things cost, and how Londoners generally spent their money. And from just a small selection of government legislation and private correspondence we would gain a pretty accurate picture of at least *some* aspects of life in 2019.

In addition to these broad-brush impressions of 21st-century London, historians of AD 4019 would have highly detailed portraits of particular individuals, some famous, some obscure. Much would be reliably said about the Prime Minister or the Queen, of course, but it would only take the chance discovery of a bundle of letters from a few individuals to be able to piece together a detailed, even intimate, account of the lives of ordinary men and women of the time.

INCOMPLETE BUT INTIMATE

Ancient history is just like this. It is both frustratingly incomplete and remarkably intimate. While we have formal biographical accounts of Tiberius, for example, as well as coins and inscriptions bearing his name and titles, we do not have even *one* piece of personal correspondence from the emperor. And, yet, from a slightly later period we have

121 letters of Pliny the Younger (nephew of the older Pliny) to various friends and colleagues, including a good number of replies from the emperor of his time (Trajan). These are a treasure trove of insights into one Roman aristocrat's thoughts, work, hunting trips, reading habits, holidaying, loves, hopes and fears.

To give an example closer to the home of the first Christians, we have solid *general* evidence that the most influential Jewish rabbi in Roman Judea was a scholar named Hillel. But sadly, we don't have a single letter from this man who was, by all accounts, an intellectual *tour de force* of the movement known as the Pharisees.

By contrast, we have close to 30,000 words of correspondence from a junior Pharisee (just a few decades after Hillel) named Saul of Tarsus. He is better known as the apostle Paul, the author of numerous letters now contained in the New Testament. These letters, while chiefly read today for their theological content, offer an enormous amount of random information about first-century language, rhetoric, religion, social history, travel and customs (Jewish, Greek and Roman), as well as the inner life of one Jewish-born, Greek-educated man responsible for taking the Christian message throughout Asia Minor (Turkey), Greece, and beyond.

We could multiply examples like this for the remainder of the book, but the point is probably clear enough. The historic past is a genuine place on the map of human experience—as real as the coin around my neck—and while much will never be known about ancient Rome or Jerusalem, more than enough documents and artefacts have survived from the period for us to offer firm judgements about many things from the first century, including things that are the focus of this book.

HOW WE KNOW WHAT WE KNOW

Just as the Roman writers Tacitus and Suetonius left us good biographical material about Tiberius, at least four individuals wrote biographies of Jesus of Nazareth. Again, just as the numerous Latin letters of Pliny the Younger provide remarkable insight into the life and thought of a well-connected Roman and his friends, so also a handful of Greek letters penned by Saul-turned-Paul offer early detailed evidence of the beginnings of what would come to be called "Christianity".

There is no difference between these two examples, in terms of historical method and judgement. The difference is simply that historical statements about Pliny come with no psychological or moral baggage. Who cares that Pliny, for example, recommended taking books when hunting in the forest in case you got bored? Historical judgements about the figure of Jesus, on the other hand, while just as easy to make as judgements about Pliny, come with all sorts of awkward baggage about God, the good life, heaven and hell, and all that!

The trick is to make our historical evaluation without letting our psychological or moral sensibilities either get in the way or carry us away. Just because we might not happen to believe in, say, "sin" or "God" does not mean we should doubt the evidence that Jesus spoke about sin and taught that God offers us forgiveness.

A BOOK OF HISTORY

This is a book of history. It is an attempt to explain *how* we know about an ancient figure like Jesus or Paul, and also something of *what* we know. I use the word "know" deliberately. The conclusions of history, including the history of Jesus, are *known*. This is why history itself used to be called a "science", from the Latin *scientia* or "knowledge". It is a straightforward fact that those specialising in this period, regardless of religious affiliation or none, agree overwhelmingly that we *know* a fair bit about Jesus. The conclusion of Duke University's E.P. Sanders in his classic book *The Historical Figure of Jesus* would be acceptable to most secular experts in the field today:

> *There are no substantial doubts about the general course of Jesus' life: when and where he lived, approximately when and where he died, and the sort of thing that he did during his public activity.*[3]

Sanders is no friend of Christian apologetics or of theology dressed up as history. As one of the leaders of the *secular* approach to studying Jesus over the last 30 years, Sanders has no qualms about dismissing this or that bit of the New Testament. Yet, he rightly regards the Gospels and the letters of Paul as important *human* sources, crucial for a good understanding of the events in Roman Galilee and Judea in the 20s and 30s AD, the time when Tiberius reigned, when his mother Livia passed away, when Pliny (Elder) was learning to read, and when the coin around my neck was struck.

In A Nutshell

Historical events were once as real as the experiences you are having today. Indeed, they are no different from the events of yesterday. Those events are no longer here—in a sense, nothing but the immediate present is "here"—but they are solid facts of the same world we inhabit. Historical investigation is

---

3   E.P. Sanders, *The Historical Figure of Jesus* (Penguin Books, 1993), p 11.

the science and art of discerning how much of those tangible events of the past can be *known* today.

Readings

Jesus and the denarius, from the Gospel of Mark

Later they sent some of the Pharisees and Herodians to Jesus to catch him in his words. They came to him and said, "Teacher, we know that you are a man of integrity. You aren't swayed by others, because you pay no attention to who they are; but you teach the way of God in accordance with the truth. Is it right to pay the imperial tax to Caesar or not? Should we pay or shouldn't we?" But Jesus knew their hypocrisy. "Why are you trying to trap me?" he asked. "Bring me a denarius and let me look at it." They brought the coin, and he asked them, "Whose image is this? And whose inscription?" "Caesar's," they replied. Then Jesus said to them, "Give back to Caesar what is Caesar's and to God what is God's." And they were amazed at him.   MARK 12 v 13-17

The historical setting of the Gospel of Luke

In the fifteenth year of the reign of Tiberius Caesar—when Pontius Pilate was governor of Judea, Herod tetrarch of Galilee, his brother Philip tetrarch of Iturea and Traconitis, and Lysanias tetrarch of Abilene—during the high-priesthood of Annas and Caiaphas, the word of God came to John son of

Zechariah in the wilderness. He went into all the country around the Jordan, preaching a baptism of repentance for the forgiveness of sins. LUKE 3 v 1-3

A letter of the Roman governor Pliny the Younger to his wife Calpurnia

You cannot believe how much I miss you. I love you so much, and we are not used to separations. So I stay awake most of the night thinking of you, and by day I find my feet carrying me (a true word, carrying) to your room at the times I've usually visited you; then finding it empty I depart, as sick and sorrowful as a lover locked out. The only time I am free from this misery is when I am in court and wearing myself out with my friends' lawsuits. You can judge then what a life I am leading, when I find my rest in work and distraction in trouble and anxiety.

Pliny, *Letters, 6*

"Faith"
in history

In the last 24 hours I have placed my faith in a host of situations. When I woke up yesterday, the radio news told me about some terrible mudslides in California. I haven't seen the pictures, but I believe the story—I have faith in the reports.

I also believed it when my daughter rang me in the middle of the day to say that she was out for a run and suddenly felt terribly ill on the side of the road. I had no evidence she was telling the truth, but I raced out the door to pick her up anyway. In the afternoon, my best mates, Ben and Karen, flew out of Sydney back to the UK—or so they told me. I didn't ask to see their plane tickets or printed itinerary, but I gave them a hug and a kiss goodbye in good faith, and promised to catch up when I'm back in Oxford in May. They seemed to believe me about that, too.

Then last night—it was an eventful day—I was out to dinner with friends when I received a call from a colleague informing me that the six-year-old daughter of a family from church had just passed away a few hours earlier. I jumped straight into "minister-mode" and made the appropriate calls, texts, and sad arrangements.

As I fell into bed around 11 p.m., I listened to a podcast and learned some trivial details—everything felt trivial after my earlier call—about Donald Trump's style of negotiation in recent talks with the Democrats over immigration policy. I woke up this morning still *believing* everything I took on faith yesterday. And I feel none the worse for it. In fact, I shudder to think how the day might have panned out had I not accepted things on faith—had I instead demanded to see observable evidence before believing anyone!

EVERYDAY FAITH

My guess is that you—and most of my readers—have accepted *on faith* everything I just wrote (I assure you it is all true, not a convenient illustration that authors make up to add spice to their books). But why would you believe me? We have never met. If you have never read anything of mine before, I am just some random Australian with a passion for history.

So, what is going on here, with *my faith* in the various reports of the last 24 hours, and *your faith* in my reporting of those reports? The answer is simple: *through long experience of interacting with others in the world, we have come to think that it is wise, most of the time, to put a good measure of trust in the testimony of others, when those people seem to be giving that testimony in good faith.* Because exercising "faith" has a proven track record of leading you to information about the real world, you have come to treat *faith in testimony* as a generally reliable bridge to personal knowledge.

TRUSTING TESTIMONY

Faith in testimony is crucial for *academic* knowledge, as well as personal knowledge. Virtually everything we learned at school or university we took on faith. We *trusted the testimony* of the teacher because we didn't have direct knowledge of any of the things in the curriculum. In English class, we trusted what was said about Shakespeare: when he lived, which plays are his, and the correct jargon for the literary devices he employs (soliloquy, *double entendre* and so on).

The same is true of the history class. Every single thing we say we "know" about the Norman invasion of Saxon England in 1066—even the date itself—we know only because we judged that it was reasonable to trust the teacher and the textbook. Even in the science classroom, virtually everything we accepted as true about cell biology, the speed of light, quantum mechanics and so on, we embraced, and still do, purely and simply on faith—trust in the knowledge and good intentions of teachers and texts.

This is even true among professional scientists across the disciplines. Biologists, for example, *trust* what their colleagues in astrophysics tell them about the cosmos, without laboriously repeating all their observations and checking their maths in detail. In the same way, the astrophysicists trust the biologists on the mechanics of the cell, without needing to go anywhere near a microscope. This is just as true for me as a researcher of the ancient world. I have direct knowledge only of some things—the languages, texts, names and archaeology of Roman Judaea and Galilee—but for most of the rest of Graeco-Roman history I gratefully rely on the published findings (the testimony) of other researchers.[4]

---

4   For a detailed account of the indispensability of trust in life and in academia, see the fabulous book by philosopher Tony Coady of the University of Melbourne: C. A. J. Coady, *Testimony: A Philosophical Study* (Clarendon Press, 1995).

THE LIMITS OF TESTIMONY AND FAITH

However, there are times when human testimony is flawed or malicious. Someone we thought was a trustworthy expert turns out to be badly mistaken or wildly overconfident in their claims. A friend (or former friend) who swore blind that something was true turns out to be a barefaced liar. Experiences like these dent our trust, our faith, in the testimony of others. They leave us with a heightened sensitivity to the possibility of human untrustworthiness and our own gullibility.

And that's fine—it's even good.

Hopefully, these experiences leave us with clues about how to distinguish between good testimony and bad, leaving us a little less vulnerable to false witness next time. Five-year-olds might trust everything they are told by grown-ups, but 30-somethings have usually learned to be more cautious. They instinctively look for signs of falsehood. They might even unconsciously apply a few simple tests to judge the internal coherence of someone's testimony and the general reliability of the person testifying (a rudimentary form of "historical method"). But in both cases—for the innocent child and the experienced adult—a general dependence on testimony is a *must* in life. Faith is a sturdy bridge to knowledge.

SCEPTICAL DEFINITIONS

The sceptical definition of "faith" as *believing things without evidence* really only made it into our dictionaries because of recent usage in sceptical circles. That is how dictionaries work. They are not arbiters of the best use of terms. They record how people end up using words. And only relatively late in its history (in the 19th century) did the word "faith" come to be used, by some, in the derogatory sense of *believing things with no good reason.* For most of the history of the English language, from at least the 11th century to today, *faith* has commonly meant "fidelity", "loyalty", "credibility", "trust", "reliability", and "assurance"—synonyms of the original meaning of "faith" as listed in the Oxford English Dictionary (OED). Two definitions of faith from this entry in the OED in particular provide a perfect explanation of why faith is essential to knowledge in general, and to *historical* knowledge in particular:

> 7(a) *Firm trust or belief in or reliance upon something (e.g. the truth of a statement or doctrine; the ability, goodness, etc., of a person, the efficacy or worth of a thing); confidence; credence.*
>
> 7(b) *Belief based on evidence, testimony, or authority.*

The point of all this for our investigation into history, and the history of Jesus of Nazareth in particular, is that our common-sense *trust in testimony*, which underlies much of our personal and academic knowledge of the world, is also crucial for gaining knowledge *about the past*. To *do history* involves reading and reflecting on ancient testimony, and deciding whether to rely on it or reject it (or something in between). We approach ancient testimony—the "primary sources" explored in the coming chapters—in much the same way we approach testimony in ordinary life. Historians ask questions like these:

- Was the author in a good position to know the information reported?

- Does the author have the general character of someone reporting in good faith?

- Does what is reported fit with what is known more broadly about the time and place spoken of?

- Are any of the specific things the author reports corroborated, at least in broad terms, by the testimony of other authors?

THE PSYCHOLOGY OF FAITH AND DOUBT

Belief and doubt are *psychological* realities just as much as they are intellectual conditions. The first thinker to probe the *psychology of belief*—so far as we know—was the Greek philosopher Aristotle (384-322 BC). He wrote what is arguably the most successful textbook in history, on any subject. His *The Art of Rhetoric* was studied in universities around the world, from the ancient Academy of Athens through to the late medieval universities of Paris and Oxford, right up to the early modern period in places like Harvard and Princeton. The book is a detailed analysis of why some arguments work and others do not—or, more accurately, why we find ourselves persuaded by some people and not by others.

Aristotle offers three terms for the three parts of persuasion:

1. The logical dimension he calls *logos*.

2. The ethical aspect (that is, whether the persuader appears morally credible) he calls *ethos*.

3. And the emotional dimension he calls *pathos*.

Each of these aspects of persuasion can be divided into numerous subcategories, but the basic idea is that persuasion works, or doesn't, because of a range of factors, not just the facts.

For better or worse, we are not brains suspended in a solution. Instead, we interpret information based on our preferences and past experiences. We are influenced by the opinions of those we admire. We cannot help but be motivated (or led astray) by concrete things like age, health, sleep patterns, and even what we ate this morning. In other words, we are not *pure mind*. We are also social, psychological and bodily creatures. This has significant implications for how we all approach evidence.

KNOW THYSELF

The wisdom of knowing one's own cognitive and emotional influences is the core insight of one of my favourite books of the last decade, the *New York Times* bestselling *The Righteous Mind: Why Good People Are Divided by Politics and Religion* (Vintage, 2013) by Jonathan Haidt. Professor Haidt is an evolutionary social psychologist from New York University.

The book is an account of the last 20 years of research into how we form (and defend) our beliefs about politics, religion, ethics, aesthetics and even science. Study after study shows that we tend to make up our minds *intuitively*, and only then prop up our positions with rational argumentation.

This powerful insight cuts all ways. It is true of both conservatives and progressives, of both fundamentalists and sceptics. Some of the evidence for the conclusion is hilarious—I thoroughly recommend the book—but the simple, recurrent lesson is that belief and unbelief are usually the result of a mix of factors. Rational argumentation plays a part. But a significant role (the *main* role, if Haidt is correct) is played by the preferences and life experiences that make up our "intuitive cognition", as he calls it. Haidt remarks:

> We ask *"Can* I believe it?" when we *want* to believe something, but *"Must* I believe it?" when we *don't want* to believe. The answer is almost always "yes" to the first question and "no" to the second.

IT DOESN'T MATTER HOW CLEVER YOU ARE

Perhaps most interesting, even scary, is the evidence described by Haidt showing that high-IQ individuals are no better than average-IQ individuals at assessing the range of arguments on both sides of a matter. Tests reveal that the only "edge" high-IQ people have is the ability to rationalise their opinions to themselves and argue their positions with others. They have what Haidt calls an "in-house press secretary" who can automatically justify everything. "People with higher IQs are able to generate more reasons" for their side of a debate, he says, "but they are no better than others at finding reasons on the other side". Smart folk are simply better at winning arguments—with themselves and others.

The research Haidt outlines perhaps explains the much-touted conclusion that atheists are generally more intelligent than those who believe in God.[5] If Haidt is right that intelligence merely enables people to argue themselves (and others) into a viewpoint, we may conclude that smart folk are better at arguing *away* the evidence for God. Their intelligence says nothing about the quality of the evidence itself. I intend no offence to atheists in saying any of this.

Indeed, the same research can be turned around to bite certain Christians. When we break the data down, it turns out that while atheists, *broadly speaking,* tend to be more intelligent than theists, Anglicans (the Church of England or Episcopalians) tend to have the highest IQs of the lot—yes, they have more intelligence than atheists (see the Nyborg study just cited). What does this mean? In light of Jonathan Haidt's point about the link between intelligence and rationalisation, probably not much. Both atheists and Anglicans

---

5   See, for example, Helmuth Nyborg, "The intelligence–religiosity nexus: A representative study of white adolescent Americans", *Intelligence* 37.1, 2009, p 81-93.

should resist the temptation to cite their IQ scores as confirmation of the things they believe. They may just be better at convincing themselves they're right!

None of these insights about belief and doubt are rocket science. We probably detect the same things all around us, and in ourselves, on a daily basis. The importance of being conscious of it, however, especially when exploring a subject like the history of Jesus, is simply to note that *evidence* will not be the only factor at play as we assess the relevant material. Intellectual examination will rightly play a central role, but so will our feelings about the man from Nazareth, our previous experience of Christians, and, frankly, whether or not we warm to the author we happen to be reading. The key in all of this is simply to be aware of ourselves, in all our human complexity.

In A Nutshell

"Faith" is not the opposite of knowledge. Trusting human testimony is fundamental both to living in the world and to learning about the past. And this *trust*, like *doubt*, can be influenced by psychological and social factors, just as much as by intellectual considerations.

Readings

Testimony about Jesus in the Gospel of John

Peter turned and saw that the disciple whom Jesus loved was following them. (This was the one who had leaned back against Jesus at the supper and had said, "Lord, who is going to betray you?") ... This is the disciple who testifies to these things and who wrote them down. We know that his testimony is true. Jesus did many other things as well. If every one of them were written down, I suppose that even the whole world would not have room for the books that would be written.   JOHN 21 v 20-25

Testimony about the eruption of Mount Vesuvius from Pliny the Younger

We had scarcely set down to rest when darkness fell: not the darkness of a moonless or cloudy night, but as if the lamp had been put out in a closed room. You could hear the shrieks of women, the wailing of infants, and the shouting of men; some calling their parents, others their children or their wives, trying to recognise them by their voices. People bewailed their own fate or that of their relatives, and there were some who prayed for death in their terror of dying. Many besought the aid of the gods, but still more imagined there were no gods left and that the universe was plunged into eternal darkness forevermore ... We were terrified to see everything changed, buried deep in ashes like snowdrifts. We returned to Misenum (just West of Naples) where we attended to our physical needs as best we could, and then spent an anxious night alternating between hope and fear.   Pliny, *Letters* 6.20

How to make me
eat my Bible

O n 18th December a few years ago, friends and colleagues alerted me to an article in the mainstream
press suggesting that the history of Jesus was entirely dubi-
ous. *You can almost set your clock by it—Christmas is upon us,*
I thought.

But this was different. Social media was alight with
shares and retweets, because this piece appeared in the
venerable *Washington Post*, and seemed to go further than
the usual polite debunking of this or that element of the
Nativity story. The author concluded triumphantly in the
final line, "In sum, there are clearly good reasons to doubt
Jesus' historical existence—if not to think it outright im-
probable."[6]

Imagine my surprise when I discovered that the author of
the article had been a recent student of mine on the course
I teach on "Historical Jesus to Written Gospels" for the
University of Sydney. This young man had sat through lec-

---

6   www.washingtonpost.com/posteverything/wp/2014/12/18/did-historical-jesus-
     exist-the-traditional-evidence-doesnt-hold-up/?hpid=z2&utm_term=.75c39646f78f

tures that outlined the sources used by scholars, the latest historical methods, and the broad conclusions of the scholarly consensus in this large field of study.

It turns out that this student was an active ex-Christian atheist doing a PhD in another department of the university (Religious Studies) critiquing the well-known Christian author and scholar William Lane Craig. Around the same time he self-published a book entitled *There Was No Jesus, There is No God.*

Given the student's clear commitment to a cause, I didn't feel too bad that I had failed to convince him just how idiosyncratic it is in secular scholarship to propose the non-existence of Jesus of Nazareth. He was like an anti-vaxxer or flat-earther disdaining mainstream science. With a wave of his hand he dismissed what he called the "atrocious methods" of historians of Jesus. No offence taken. I was glad to have the opportunity to offer a reply to my student's claims.[7]

But my main point here is not the historical particulars—we have plenty of time to explore those in this book. I want to make the observation that scepticism can sometimes be as dogmatic as fundamentalism. They can be the mirror-image of each other.

ISSUING THE CHALLENGE

In what might turn out to be a rush of blood to the head, a few years ago I was so confident that Jesus' existence is regarded as beyond reasonable doubt in contemporary secular scholarship that I published a challenge on the ABC (Australia's public broadcaster): if anyone can find *just one* full professor of Ancient History, Classics, or New Testament in

---

7   abc.net.au/religion/articles/2014/12/24/4154120.htm (accessed 4th June 2019).

any real university anywhere in the world who argues that Jesus never lived, I will eat a page out of my Bible.[8]

The response on social media was fun, as various sceptical friends (and some who were not-so-much friends) set out to make me eat holy Scripture. As the hours and days passed, a volley of names was offered: professors of psychology, English literature, philosophy, folklore (I kid you not), and German language—but *not one* professor from any of the relevant fields. My Bible was safe.

I have since inadvertently discovered that there is an atheist group here in Australia determined to meet the challenge. And when they find an eligible professor who denies the historical existence of Jesus, the intention is apparently to barge into my office with a camera and make me eat a page of my Bible for the online public to enjoy live.

A SHORTCUT TO THE SCHOLARLY CONSENSUS

Whether or not there is an eligible professor out there who denies Jesus ever lived, there is a simple shortcut for non-specialists to confirm that there is, indeed, a consensus among contemporary *secular* scholars that the broad outline of Jesus' life is historically sound. This does not *prove* that Jesus existed, but it does demonstrate that professional scholarship—even outside religious institutions—considers there to be no real doubt about his existence.

Anyone with access to a serious public or university library can easily consult the standard reference works in the disciplines of ancient history and classics. The big academic publishing houses produce compendiums designed to describe the state-of-the-question on all things historical.

---

8 abc.net.au/news/2014-10-17/dickson-ill-eat-a-page-from-my-bible-if-jesus-didnt-exist/5820620 (accessed 4th June 2019).

There are at least *five* such works that would be regarded as the authoritative and relevant volumes in English-speaking secular academia.

FIVE EXAMPLES OF CONSENSUS

The first is the famous single-volume *Oxford Classical Dictionary* (published by Oxford University Press), which summarises scholarship on all things Greek and Roman in just a little over 1,700 pages. The several-page entry on the origins of Christianity begins with an assessment of what may be reliably known about Jesus of Nazareth. Readers will discover that no doubts are raised about the basic facts: that this teacher-healer really lived and really did die by crucifixion.

Next is the much larger *Cambridge Ancient History* in 14 volumes (published, of course, by Cambridge University Press). Volume 10 covers the Augustan period, right about when Tiberius, Livia, Pliny the Elder and Jesus all lived. It has a sizeable chapter on the birth of Christianity. The entry begins with a couple of pages outlining what is known of Jesus' life and death, including his preaching of the kingdom of God, his fraternising with sinners and so on. No doubts are raised about the authenticity of these core elements of the Jesus story.

The third relevant standard work is also published by Cambridge University in the UK. It's the *Cambridge History of Judaism* in four volumes. Volume 3 covers the early Roman period. Several different chapters refer to Jesus *in passing* as an interesting figure of Jewish history. One chapter—60 pages in length—focuses entirely on Jesus and is written by two leading scholars, neither of whom has any qualms about dismissing bits of the New Testament record when they think the evidence is against it. The chapter offers a first-rate account of what experts currently think of the historical Jesus. His teaching, fame as a healer, openness to sinners, selection of "the twelve" (apostles), prophetic actions (like cleansing the temple), clashes with elites, and, of course, his death on a cross are *all* treated as beyond reasonable doubt. The authors do not tackle the resurrection (unsurprisingly), but they do acknowledge, as a matter of historical fact, that the first disciples of Jesus...

> *...were absolutely convinced that Jesus of Nazareth had been raised and was Lord and that numerous of them were certain that he had appeared to them.*

INSCRIPTIONS

The fourth standard work comes from a different angle entirely and is very revealing for anyone who imagines there are doubts about Jesus' existence in mainstream secular scholarship. The monumental *Corpus Inscriptionum Iudaeae/ Palaestinae* (from Germany's 260-year-old publishing house De Gruyter) is a recent six-volume compendium of all the known inscriptions in Judaea/Palestine for the thousand year period from Alexander the Great to Muhammad. A photo of each inscription (when available) appears, followed by an analysis of its date, context, and content.

Some might be surprised to read entry 15 of the Jerusalem inscriptions: "Titulus on the cross of Jesus in three languages: Aramaic, Latin and Greek, ca. 30 AD". The four renditions of the inscription from the Gospels appear (basically, "Jesus of Nazareth, King of the Jews"), followed by a brief commentary on the Roman practice of placarding the reason for the punishment of a condemned person. The entry then states: "Therefore there is no reason to doubt the tradition that a *titulus* with the reason for his condemnation by Pilatus was affixed on Jesus' cross."

The point for my purposes isn't just that this volume affirms the tiny detail of the sign above Jesus' cross—that is probably of minor interest to most readers. The point is that this peerless historical compendium of ancient inscriptions takes it as *an absolute given* that the Jewish figure of Jesus existed, that he caused a scandal of some kind and that he ended up on a Roman cross.

The fifth and final example is *Brill's New Pauly: Encyclopaedia of the Ancient World* (published by Brill Academic). It is a classic German-language compendium of Ancient History, now translated into English in 20 volumes. You can buy your own set for just €5,795 (a little over £5,000 or $6,600). Of course it has an entry on the historical Jesus, reaching 5239 words (I didn't count; each entry tells you exactly how many words it contains).

It is sceptical about a lot of things in the Gospels. It has no interest in propping up the Christian faith. But nor does it express even the slightest doubt about Jesus' existence, the basic themes of his teaching, his reputation as a healer, and his crucifixion.

BEYOND DOUBT

None of these five works are theological, or even remotely religious. They are the standard secular reference works to which scholars themselves turn to double-check certain details, and to get a quick summary of the state-of-the-question for just about any ancient topic you can imagine. Each volume treats the existence of Jesus the teacher, healer, and martyr as beyond doubt.

I recognise that this chapter amounts to what philosophers

call *an argument from authority*—we have not yet begun to explore the direct evidence for Jesus. But arguments from authority are far from bogus. They are used all the time in courts of law—where the judgement of an expert witness is considered evidence. And we all rely on authorities for many of the things we *know* about the world. If, for example, I am not a particle physicist, I will have to rely on experts for pretty much everything I know about the atom. When I learn that a consensus of particle physicists agrees that the Higgs boson exists and has a mass of approximately 125 GeV/c2, I am justified in accepting this consensus as a shortcut to reliable knowledge on the topic.

It is no different with matters of history. The fact that there is an obvious consensus of scholarship that places Jesus' existence *beyond doubt* must count for something: not everything, but something.

In a Nutshell

The claim that Jesus of Nazareth did not even exist has virtually no currency in contemporary scholarship. All the standard (secular) compendiums of ancient history judge the core of the story—that a popular Galilean teacher and reputed healer named Jesus was crucified in Jerusalem by order of Pontius Pilate—to be beyond reasonable doubt.

Reading

A brief summary of the life of Jesus in a speech (by the apostle Peter) recorded in the book of Acts

Peter said, "You know the message God sent to the people of Israel, announcing the good news of peace through Jesus Christ, who is Lord of all. You know what has happened throughout the province of Judea, beginning in Galilee after the baptism that John preached—how God anointed Jesus of Nazareth with the Holy Spirit and power, and how he went around doing good and healing all who were under the power of the devil, because God was with him. We are witnesses of everything he did in the country of the Jews and in Jerusalem. They killed him by hanging him on a cross, but God raised him from the dead on the third day and caused him to be seen. He was not seen by all the people, but by witnesses whom God had already chosen—by us who ate and drank with him after he rose from the dead. He commanded us to preach to the people and to testify that he is the one whom God appointed as judge of the living and the dead. All the prophets testify about him that everyone who believes in him receives forgiveness of sins through his name."

ACTS 10 v 36-43

Historical quests
for Jesus

The last two centuries have seen many shifting scholarly judgements about the figure of Jesus before arriving at something *approximating* a consensus today about the general course of his life. This is true of many academic disciplines.

The journey of science toward confident judgements about the world is the result of a huge amount of new information and much better investigative tools. In a similar way, the quest for the historical Jesus has benefited from numerous discoveries and greatly improved methods over many generations of critical discussion. And perhaps the best-kept secret of all is that this academic discipline has not become *more* sceptical of Jesus' life but less.

The fact that many among the general public still have the impression that scholars think we know little about Jesus is really just a function of the way culture is often 30 years behind academia. Textbooks often speak of three phases in research—three "quests"—into the life of Jesus.

THE FIRST QUEST: THE RATIONALIST JESUS

The first of these quests for Jesus was born in the Enlightenment, that Europe-wide movement of the 17th and 18th centuries which broke away from the traditions of the past, whether the philosophy of Aristotle or the dogma of the church. Instead, it emphasised individual human powers of *reason* to discover what is true about the world. This celebration of reason soon directed its attention to the central figure of Western culture to that point: Jesus of Nazareth.

Leading the charge to challenge the "traditional" Jesus and uncover the supposedly original historical figure was a professor from Hamburg, Germany, named Hermann Samuel Reimarus (1694-1768). He had long harboured reservations about Christian doctrine. He thought there was probably a God but only in the sense of a distant Mind behind the rational order of creation. He did not believe God entered the world in Jesus to save us and take us to some ethereal "kingdom come". In his *Apologia or Defence of the Rational Worshippers of God* he proposed that Jesus was little more than an anti-Roman Jewish rebel whose followers later elevated him to spiritual "Saviour". The modern contrast you sometimes hear about between "the Jesus of history" and "the Christ of faith" comes from Reimarus.

A different tack was taken by another German Enlightenment thinker named David Friedrich Strauss (1808-1874). Rather than describe the Gospels as deceptions, Strauss suggested these texts can be read as "myth". He did not simply mean they were *false*. He meant that the Gospels were metaphorical accounts of the religious impact of Jesus. Jesus did not *actually* give sight to the blind—every good Enlightenment thinker *knew* that miracles do not happen! Such stories were, Strauss argued, intended to remind readers of the spiritual health, or insight, we can gain from Christ. His work *The Life of Jesus Critically Examined* was one of the most popular books of the 19th century. Its impact is still felt today whenever people suggest that the Gospels are parables of spiritual truth rather than biographies of a real life.

One further Enlightenment academic is worth mentioning (there were dozens who explored Jesus from this rationalist perspective). Joseph Ernest Renan (1823-1892) was a French historian and philosopher. He published his *Life of Jesus* in 1863, and the work can probably be credited with the still hugely popular idea that Jesus was a simple, beautiful teacher of ethics, not an authoritative messianic figure.

THE DEATH OF THE RATIONALIST JESUS

All of these portraits of Jesus—whether as a political rebel, a symbol of the higher life or a simple ethical teacher—have two things in common. First, their authors did not apply any discernible historical method to the source material (the Gospels). Each scholar simply included some evidence and excluded other evidence. There was little attempt to do what historians now consider the basis of all good history: read the entire testimony in the Gospels in light of all that is known from other sources about the setting from which the testimony comes (more about that later).

Had Reimarus followed this now-typical course, he would have noted how difficult it is to make Jesus fit the pattern of a Jewish freedom-fighter. Had Strauss read the Gospels against the wider literature of the first century, he would have seen how closely the Gospels align *not* with the mythical literature of the period but with the numerous historical biographies of the day. And had Renan accessed the wider Jewish materials from the era, he would have observed how well Jesus' theology and eschatology (that is, ideas about a future *coming kingdom*) resonated with the hopes of many in his day, and how his ethical teachings cannot be understood apart from that eschatological theology.

The second thing that such portraits have in common is that, on closer inspection, they all read like (unconscious) efforts to *project* onto a first-century figure the ethics and philosophy of the 18th- and 19th-century Enlightenment. They were wish-fulfilments. And it fell to a colossus of early 20th-century academia to point this out, and so bring down the entire Enlightenment search for Jesus in one humble volume. The book was titled *The Quest of the Historical Jesus,* and its author was Albert Schweitzer (1875-1965).

THE END OF THE FIRST QUEST

Albert Schweitzer was a freak of intellect. He held a doctorate in philosophy, another in theology, and later picked up a medical degree. After gaining a reputation as the foremost authority on the music of J.S. Bach (and as an expert organist), Schweitzer turned his considerable powers of analysis to the study of Jesus. He published several groundbreaking volumes on Christianity, but it was his book on Jesus that had the most impact. It is no exaggeration to say that in the field of Christian origins Schweitzer was an Albert Einstein figure: things could not be the same after him.

Schweitzer's *The Quest of the Historical Jesus* came out in 1906.[9] It was mostly a stinging critique of the previous 150 years of scholarship, including that of Reimarus, Strauss, Renan, and many others. It called on experts to give more serious attention to the ancient sources themselves, and to

---

9   Originally published in German, of course, a standard English version is *The Quest of the Historical Jesus* (Dover Publications, 2005).

stop allowing their "preferred Jesus" to determine what evidence was included, and how that evidence was handled. The Jesus of the Enlightenment, he concluded, was little more than "a figure designed by rationalism, endowed with life by liberalism, and clothed by modern theology in an historical garb" (p 396). This "Jesus", in other words, was really just a rationalist, and equally dogmatic, counter-theology to replace the dogmatic theology of the church.

Schweitzer himself offered only a meagre portrait of Jesus—what he called a "sketch". And no one could accuse him of projecting his own preferences onto the ancient Galilean. In Schweitzer's analysis, Jesus was an "eschatological prophet" who forewarned Israel of impending doom and called on people to find shelter from the coming judgment *in himself.* Thus his death (which, Schweitzer was adamant, Jesus himself intended and provoked) was a conscious attempt to bear in himself the great catastrophe coming upon the world, so that at least a few people—his disciples—would avoid judgment and enter a new world order: the "kingdom of God". I reread Schweitzer just before writing this paragraph; it is provocative stuff!

Schweitzer admitted that he did not know what to do with this eschatological Jesus. His portrait was not as *timeless* as Strauss' mythic story of spiritual insight; nor was it as immediately *relevant* as Renan's charming Galilean ethicist. But it was *historical.* That is what Schweitzer was aiming for. He was willing to sacrifice the personal religious significance of Jesus for an accurate account of his life and aims. "The historical Jesus will be to our time a stranger and an enigma", he lamented (p 397).

It is unclear if Schweitzer maintained the Christian faith of his youth—his father had been a Lutheran minister. He soon gave up his scholarly career and became a doctor among lepers in Gabon, West Africa. When I visited his family home, now a museum, in Kaysersberg (now part of France) a few years ago, I couldn't help looking at all the ponderous, almost grave, photos of him from a century ago and wondering what he really thought about Jesus, beyond his "sketch".

Astonishingly, Schweitzer's portrait of the eschatological prophet warning of judgment and calling on people to flee to the safety of his vision of the kingdom has largely stood the test of time. In fact, with the discovery in the 1940s and 50s of thousands of Jewish texts in caves by the Dead Sea—the famous Dead Sea Scrolls—as well as hundreds of archaeological finds in Galilee and Judaea over the last few decades, this basic eschatological account of Jesus is the only one that commands wide agreement across the scholarly spectrum today. I wish Schweitzer was alive to see how, because of new evidence and methods, his humble "sketch" has grown into a marvellous tapestry of historical knowledge.

If Albert Schweitzer brought down what we call the "first quest" for Jesus (the Enlightenment search), he also set the stage for the vast scholarly programme known today as the "third quest" for Jesus.

THE SECOND QUEST FOR JESUS

You may be wondering what happened in the "*second* quest" for Jesus. Not a lot. For the 50 years after Schweitzer, scholars were nervous about exploring the historical Jesus. Not only had Schweitzer unsettled scholars with the realisation that it is easy to *project* onto Jesus our own cultural preferences, but his sketch left people scratching their heads about the usefulness of an eschatological prophet for philosophy, theology, ethics, or culture. As a result, the number of works on the historical Jesus between 1906 and the 1950s dropped dramatically.

What we call the second quest for Jesus was a highly cautious attempt (from the mid 1950s) to establish some basic facts about the man from Nazareth. Its results and impact were limited. It was also led astray by a new historical methodology dubbed the "criterion of double dissimilarity". This approach affirmed that material in the Gospels which does not sound Jewish or Christian probably came from the historical Jesus himself. The reasoning was simple: the writers of the Gospels were unlikely to invent material that did not fit with their Jewish background or with the later teachings of their churches. So things that are "dissimilar" from Judaism and Christianity would not have been made up.

But, as many have since pointed out, that's like trying to uncover the *real* Winston Churchill by excluding anything about Great Britain or Englishness before and after the great wartime prime minister.

THE THIRD QUEST FOR JESUS

The second quest for Jesus was quickly surpassed by what is now called the third quest. Third-questers (the vast majority of the thousands of experts today) strive to do what second-questers hesitated to do (even avoided doing): interpret Jesus *against the backdrop of all that we know about Jewish culture* in the Roman period.

Rather than trying to isolate *this* or *that* saying of Jesus (bits that don't sound too Jewish or Christian), third-questers follow an approach far more typical of the broader class of ancient historians today. They pay attention to all the portraits of Jesus in our various sources and assess the plausibility of those portraits by setting them against all that we know of the background of Jesus' time and place.

The starting point for all good history is determining

what *fits* and what doesn't. Even if we can never fully verify specific details of a figure's life and thought, we must aim to make a broad judgement about the general plausibility of our accounts. This is how historians investigate lives such as Alexander the Great, Cleopatra, Emperor Tiberius and the rest. And it is the starting point for studying Jesus.

Historians of Jesus are not usually interested in proving the exact details of something Jesus said or did (the way Christians embrace every word of the New Testament as divinely inspired), but nor are they quick to dismiss what they read in the Gospels, the way some sceptical folk instinctively reject what cannot be externally corroborated. Third-questers are usually more interested in determining whether what is said about (and by) Jesus in the Gospels plausibly *fits* with our wider knowledge of his time and place. If it fits, it may tentatively be included in our growing database of credible features of the Gospels' portraits of Jesus. As the database of plausible features grows, historians begin to offer hypotheses about *what kind of Jew Jesus was, what his aims might have been, why he might have got into trouble with the Jerusalem and Roman authorities,* and so on. Such hypotheses are always subjected to new evidence or better interpretations of old evidence. And, hopefully, over time, a robust picture of the historical Jesus emerges.[10]

The basic idea of the third quest, then, is to allow Jesus' words and actions as recorded in our sources to be illuminated by the politics, culture, geography, economics and religion of first-century Galilee and Judaea. Rather than wishing Jesus to be a particular kind of figure—whether a simple

---

10 The big name in the field of the philosophy and methodology of history, as it relates to the study of Jesus, is Jens Schröter of Humboldt University in Berlin: see his *From Jesus to the New Testament: Early Christian Theology and the Origin of the New Testament Canon* (Baylor University Press, 2013).

moral teacher or the Lord and Saviour of the world—good historical method submits every thought, whether sceptical or religious, to all of the evidence we have from the time. We might call this the *criterion of historical plausibility* (in fact that is exactly what some scholars call it): *To what degree does the testimony about Jesus in our direct sources (for example, the Gospels or Paul's letters) cohere or interact with the teachings and events we know to have been current in his day?*

When the level of coherence (or interaction) is high, historians tend to have confidence that the testimony is plausible. When it is low, scholars tend to be wary.

The rest of this book will unpack some of the specific findings of the third quest and offer various thoughts about the meaning of all this for today. Unlike Schweitzer, I am not so pessimistic that "the historical Jesus will be to our time a stranger and an enigma".

In A Nutshell

One hazard in the study of Jesus is the temptation to project onto him our own preferences. A great deal of early scholarship on Jesus, especially in the Enlightenment, fell headlong into this danger. But contemporary experts are not immune either. The only defence against this intellectual misstep is to pay close attention to *all* available sources—both the direct writings about Jesus and the background writings, especially *Jewish* writings, of his day.

Reading

The eschatological element of Jesus' teaching

Then Jesus began to denounce the towns in which most of his miracles had been performed, because they did not repent. "Woe to you, Chorazin! Woe to you, Bethsaida! For if the miracles that were performed in you had been performed in Tyre and Sidon, they would have repented long ago in sackcloth and ashes. But I tell you, it will be more bearable for Tyre and Sidon on the day of judgment than for you.

And you, Capernaum, will you be lifted to the heavens? No, you will go down to Hades. For if the miracles that were performed in you had been performed in Sodom, it would have remained to this day. But I tell you that it will be more bearable for Sodom on the day of judgment than for you."

At that time Jesus said, "I praise you, Father, Lord of heaven and earth, because you have hidden these things from the wise and learned, and revealed them to little children. Yes, Father, for this is what you were pleased to do. All things have been committed to me by my Father. No one knows the Son except the Father, and no one knows the Father except the Son and those to whom the Son chooses to reveal him.

Come to me, all you who are weary and burdened, and I will give you rest. Take my yoke upon you and learn from me, for I am gentle and humble in heart, and you will find rest for your souls. For my yoke is easy and my burden is light."

MATTHEW 11 v 20-30

Liberal prophet, sacrificial martyr

As I said in the previous chapter, the central feature of today's third quest for Jesus mirrors the historical method employed by historians studying other figures of the period, whether Emperor Augustus (63 BC-AD 14), Flavius Josephus (AD 37-100), or Pliny the Younger (AD 61-112).

Historians gather everything they can that relates to the geography, culture, politics and writings of the period in which the figure lived, and then read the *direct* sources concerning the figure against that background material. This allows us to judge the overall plausibility of the specific testimony about the figure. The goal is not necessarily to verify precise details or statements—though this can sometimes be done—but to test whether we are dealing with reasonable testimony or with complete fantasy, or something in between.

In this chapter, I want to offer some examples of this methodological starting point of the third quest (which I will now just call *contemporary scholarship on Jesus*). Two of the examples concern his teaching; one relates to his death.

These will hopefully make clear why even historians with no interest in privileging Christian Scripture and doctrine nonetheless agree that the basic figure presented in the early Christian sources simply cannot be a fairytale.

DISPUTES ABOUT THE SABBATH

The Gospels report that Jesus disputed with other Jewish teachers about what was considered *work* on the "Sabbath", the mandated day of rest. For Jewish believers then, as now, "keeping the Sabbath" by not working was an immensely important part of their belief and culture. But precisely what constituted "work" was hotly debated.

In response to the criticism that Jesus was conducting his ministry on the Sabbath, he remarked"

> *"If one of you has a child or an ox that falls into a well on the Sabbath day, will you not immediately pull it out?"*
> LUKE 14 v 5

His point was that it ought to be permissible to *do good* on the Sabbath.

Strictly speaking, there is no way to establish that Jesus spoke these words: we would have to find a second independent source to confirm that. But if we could verify that this was a live topic of debate among Jews in Jesus' exact time and place, we would have reasonable grounds for concluding that Luke reports *the sort of conversation* Jesus engaged in with his contemporaries. Remember, history (like life) is more fruitful if we start with an openness to human testimony. This does not mean we gullibly accept everything, but nor does it mean we declare our sources "guilty until proved innocent".

THE ESSENES

As it turns out, one major text from the Dead Sea Scrolls—written in Judea in the period immediately before Jesus—is highly relevant to these debates over the Sabbath. It is called the *Damascus Document*, and it lays out some of the rules that this community of Jews—the Essenes—lived by.

The Essenes saw themselves as the *most*-chosen of the chosen people Israel. From their perspective, most Jews were wicked. As the introduction to the *Damascus Document* puts it, "they [other Jews] sought easy interpretations, chose illusions, scrutinised loopholes", and so on. The Essenes, however, were blessed to learn the true interpretation of God's law from a mysterious "Teacher of Righteousness", perhaps the founder of their community. This teacher laid down the correct rules for Jewish life, including what to do when your livestock, or even your neighbour, fell into a pit on the Sabbath:

> *No one should help an animal give birth on the Sabbath day. And if it falls into a well or a pit, he should not take it out on the Sabbath. Any living man who falls into a place of water or into a reservoir on the Sabbath, no one should take him out with a ladder or a rope.* DAMASCUS DOCUMENT 11.13-17

It is fair to say that those who produced the Dead Sea Scrolls did not believe in "easy interpretations" or "loopholes". For them, strict interpretation was the key to the good life and the path to God's blessing.

There is a clear connection between Jesus' statements about the Sabbath and the teachings in the *Damascus Document*. People of the time were obviously debating whether assisting animals and people out of a pit or well (a fairly common accident in the ancient world) constituted "work" and was therefore banned on the Sabbath. In light of this text, it is reasonable to suggest that Jesus probably *did* engage in debates about Sabbath rules, as the Gospels say. We can probably also conclude that Jesus tended to take the more *liberal-minded* position on such matters.

Does any of this prove that Jesus spoke the exact words, "If one of you has a child or an ox that falls into a well on the Sabbath day will you not immediately pull it out"? *No.* But does it heighten the historian's confidence that the testimony of the Gospels about this sort of thing is historical? *Yes.*

PROPHET OF THE "KINGDOM COME"

Let me offer another example of setting the story of Jesus in its Jewish context. Anyone who opens a Gospel will quickly discover that the central theme of Jesus' teaching was "the kingdom of God". In the Gospel of Mark alone—usually considered the first of the Gospels to be written (in the 60s of the first century)—the expression appears 18 times, which is more than once per chapter. It is also the first thing on Jesus' lips, according to the Gospel:

> *After John [the Baptist] was put in prison, Jesus went into Galilee, proclaiming the good news of God. "The time has come," he said. "The kingdom of God has come near. Repent and believe the good news!"*
>
> MARK 1 v 14-15

According to the Gospels, "the kingdom of God" was a big deal for Jesus. But is it *historical?* Who is to say this theme was not invented later by people desperate to find in Jesus their ticket to heaven?

For one thing, the expression "kingdom of God" in the Gospels sounds more like a political revolution coming to earth than an ethereal place we all go to when we die. Subsequent theological concerns about life after death do not feature much in Jesus' teaching. His concern seems to be more about evil being overthrown and justice being established. He spoke of the destruction of one order and "the renewal of all things" (Matthew 19 v 28). In short, the "kingdom of God" is about the Almighty doing something about the mess in the world and finally demonstrating that he is King over all creation.

WHERE DID IT COME FROM?

The historical question is, *where did this theme about the kingdom of God come from, if not from later concerns about "going to heaven"?* It is fascinating that Christian leaders in the decades following Jesus, whose letters make up the bulk of the remainder of the New Testament, only mention the kingdom of God in passing. They *assume* the theme, but they hardly ever teach about it using that specific term. This suggests that the historical background to the theme of the kingdom of God is to be found *earlier* in Jesus' immediate Jewish setting.

The Old Testament, or what Jewish people call the *Tanakh* or *Torah*, only rarely uses expressions similar to "the kingdom of God". Other Jewish writings immediately before Jesus, however, *do* use the phrase, and in a similar way. The Dead Sea Scrolls contain a few important examples, but so does a very different kind of text written around the same time, just a few decades before Jesus.

The *Psalms of Solomon* is a series of poems or songs written by Jewish leaders shortly after the Romans took control of Judaea in 63 BC. The songs were not the sort of thing imperial authorities would have enjoyed, since a dominant theme was how Israel's God would soon crush the despotic "sinners" who dared to trample down Jerusalem. In place of the sinners (the Romans), God would elevate the "righteous" who will take their rightful place in the new world order. This great upheaval is called "the kingdom". The song begins:

> *Lord, you are king forevermore,*
> *for in you, O God, does our soul take pride.*
> *We hope in God our Saviour,*
> *for the strength of our God is for ever with mercy.*
> *And* ***the kingdom of our God*** *is for ever*
> *over the nations in judgment.*
> *Lord, you chose David to be king over Israel,*
> *and swore to him about his descendants forever,*
> *that his kingdom should not fail before you …*
> PSALMS OF SOLOMON 17 *emphasis mine*

This song continues in a strain of lament, and then pivots to declare that while the sinners have temporarily challenged the kingdom, they will soon be overthrown by the promised descendant of ancient King David (the Messiah):

> *See, Lord, and raise up for them their king,*
> *the son of David,*
> *to rule over your servant Israel,*
> *to destroy the unrighteous rulers,*
> *to purge Jerusalem from Gentiles,*
> *to drive out the sinners from the inheritance;*
> *to smash the arrogance of sinners like a Potters jar.*

I had the great privilege a few years ago of handling an early copy of the *Psalms of Solomon*, preserved in the ancient Syriac language. I was filming a scene for a documentary on the background to Jesus' life, and I felt like a kid in a candy shop as I felt the pages—admittedly, wearing white gloves—and wondered about the hopes and dreams of the people who sang these patriotic hymns.

REVOLUTIONARY TALK

A song like the one just quoted—composed so close in time to Jesus—gives us a good idea of how some Jews of the period thought about their predicament under the Romans and how they envisaged their future. The key expression in the opening stanza, "the kingdom of our God", has an immediate connection to Jesus' own proclamation of God's kingdom.

Regardless of later fixations about life after death and going to heaven, the teaching of Jesus about a coming kingdom was very much part of an earlier conversation in Judaea and Galilee about the problems of suffering and tyranny, and what God was going to do about it. People in Jesus' day longed for the Almighty to step in and clean up the mess of the world. The language they used for this revolution was the "kingdom of God".

Jesus' preaching, as the Gospels describe it, very much *fits* with the specific concerns of Jewish people at the turn of the first century. Of course, this does not *prove* that Jesus said the exact words, "The kingdom of God has come near. Repent and believe the good news!" But it does mean that the Gospels' emphasis on "the kingdom of God" is very much in line with what we might expect an early first-century Jewish teacher in that part of the Roman empire to be talking about.

AN OPEN KINGDOM

The quotation from the 17th song of the *Psalms of Solomon* also shines a spotlight on Jesus' radically *different* idea about the *character* of the kingdom. While we cannot confirm specific phraseology used by Jesus, we can observe a strong tendency in his teaching to say that God's kingdom is especially concerned with what you might call the "humble". Instead, of the "total war" picture of the kingdom that we find in the *Psalms of Solomon*, the Gospels repeatedly record Jesus saying things like…

> *Blessed are the poor in spirit, for theirs is the kingdom … Blessed are the meek, for they will inherit the earth.*
> MATTHEW 5 v 3-4

> *Blessed are those who are persecuted for righteousness, for theirs is the kingdom.* MATTHEW 5 v 11

> *What shall we say the kingdom of God is like, or what parable shall we use to describe it? It is like a mustard seed, which is the smallest of all seeds on earth.*
> MARK 4 v 30-31

> *Let the little children come to me, and do not hinder them, for the kingdom of God belongs to such as these. Truly I tell you, anyone who will not receive the kingdom of God like a little child will never enter it.*
> MARK 10 v 14-15

> *It is easier for a camel to go through the eye of a needle than for someone who is rich to enter the kingdom of God.* MARK 10 v 24

On occasion, Jesus even implied a reversal of the expectation that foreigners (i.e., the Romans) would be wiped out by the coming of the kingdom. Following a tender interaction with a Roman centurion, Jesus announced to his Israelite audience,

> *"I say to you that many will come from the east and*
> *the west [i.e., foreign lands], and will take their*
> *places at the feast with Abraham, Isaac and Jacob*
> *in the kingdom of heaven. But the subjects of the*
> *kingdom [the people of Israel to whom the kingdom*
> *was originally promised] will be thrown outside."*
>
> MATTHEW 8 v 11-12

Jesus' teaching about the kingdom of God not only *fits* with the broad hopes of his fellow Jews in the period; it also seems to challenge—deliberately confront—some aspects of those dreams.

If the *Psalms of Solomon* is anything to go by, as well as passages in the Dead Sea Scrolls, it is clear that some Jewish people at the time wanted God's kingdom to come in a tornado of judgment upon the sinners of the world. Jesus, however, promised a tiny "mustard seed" that would grow slowly, humbly and almost imperceptibly, and which would one day also include people "from the east and the west". The kingdom of God, according to Jesus, was not the business of freedom-fighters eager to crush their pagan overlords. In light of his call to "love your enemies" and turn the other cheek, it is likely he thought that violence on behalf of the kingdom ruled people *out* of God's plans. The kingdom was for the "meek", the "little children" and any who welcomed its arrival with humility.

Jesus' liberal attitude to Sabbath rules and his prophet-like proclamation of the kingdom of God are widely accepted in contemporary scholarship as historically sound. These themes *fit* with what we know of his time and place. And there is no reason to doubt in these cases that the Gospels have preserved broadly accurate testimony about him.

THE LAST SUPPER

Another example of the methodological starting point for assessing Jesus concerns his death—and in particular how he viewed his death. Many capable scholars are sceptical about the occasional references in the Gospels to Jesus foretelling his own demise; such predictions sound too much like "fake prophecies", they say, retrojected into the story. But the account of Jesus' final meal, known as the Last Supper, offers substantial evidence that Jesus took a view about his impending death. Here is the scene as it appears in the earliest Gospel:

> *While they were eating, Jesus took bread, and when he had given thanks, he broke it and gave it to his disciples, saying, "Take it; this is my body." Then he took a cup, and when he had given thanks, he gave it to them, and they all drank from it. This is my blood of the covenant, which is poured out for many," he said to them. "Truly I tell you, I will not drink again from the fruit of the vine until that day when I drink it new in the kingdom of God."* MARK 14 v 22-25

There are several internal indications that these words fit comfortably in a Jewish setting. The expression "blood of the covenant" is a well-known Israelite concept, as is the reference to drinking "the fruit of the vine" in the kingdom of God. More important than that—for the historian—is that this passage is one of the few where Jesus' actual *wording* can, in part, be corroborated by a separate source. The same scene, with *nearly* identical phrasing, appears in a letter written by Paul to Corinth around the year AD 56:

60

The Lord Jesus, on the night he was betrayed, took
bread, and when he had given thanks, he broke it and
said, "This is my body, which is for you; do this in
remembrance of me." In the same way, after supper he
took the cup, saying, "This cup is the new covenant
in my blood; do this, whenever you drink it, in
remembrance of me."   I CORINTHIANS 11 v 23-25

Both the Gospel of Mark and Paul's letter to the Corinthians *now* appear in the New Testament, but the two texts were originally composed *independently* of each other. Mark was not reliant on Paul's letter, and Paul certainly did not know the Gospel of Mark. It was not until decades later that these documents were collected into a single volume which we call the New Testament.

These two accounts of the Last Supper, then, must be recognised as two independent mid-first-century versions of the same basic testimony about Jesus' final meal. Here we are about as close to corroborating the specific words of Jesus as we are for any other figure of the period (with the exception of imperial decrees). Jesus said that his broken "body" and spilt "blood" were a "(new) covenant" offered not for himself as a simple martyrdom but "for you" as a sacrifice. The frequently sceptical scholar Ed Sanders of Duke University remarks:

The passage [about the Last Supper] has the strongest
possible support … The saying makes it highly probable
that Jesus knew that he was a marked man." [11]

But the more significant question is, *how could a first-century Jew possibly describe his own death in sacrificial language*

---

11 E.P. Sanders, *The Historical Figure of Jesus.* (Penguin, 1993), p 263.

like this? The words "blood poured out" are the sort of thing the Old Testament (or Jewish Scriptures) says of the sacrifices *in the Jerusalem Temple*, where it refers to the blood of a lamb or goat "poured out" for the sins of Israel. Ancient Judaism knew nothing of *human* sacrifice for sins.

Or did it?

Further evidence puts a very different spin on things.

SACRIFICE

There is an interesting Jewish text written long *after* the Old Testament, but right around the time of Jesus, that makes clear how the atoning language of temple sacrifices could be applied to the deaths of righteous men and women. The document is known as *4 Maccabees*.

It praises Jewish martyrs who had endured horrendous torture for their faith two centuries earlier when the land of Judaea was occupied and ruled by the despotic Syro-Greek king Antiochus Epiphanes IV (215-163 BC). The work is mainly philosophical in nature but it recalls these awful historical events in order to inspire readers to remain true to the commandments of God and not give up hope in the face of new pagan masters (the Romans).

The central story of *4 Maccabees* concerns the torture and deaths of a priest named Eleazar, his wife and their seven sons. This family endured beatings, scourging, eye-gouging, and finally death in a variety of horrific ways, for not renouncing their Jewish faith. At one point, the mother…

> *…watched the flesh of her children being consumed by fire, their toes and fingers scattered on the ground, and the flesh of the head to the chin exposed like masks.*
> 4 MACCABEES 15 v 15

I will spare you any further gory details, because the key significance of this text (for my purposes) isn't the events themselves—which may or may not be accurate—but the perspective of the first-century Jewish author of *4 Maccabees*. He sees the suffering of this righteous family as an atoning sacrifice for Israel's failures. When he nears the conclusion of his story, he announces:

> *These then, having consecrated themselves for the sake of God, are now honored not only with this distinction [eternal life] but also by the fact that through them our enemies did not prevail against our nation, and the tyrant was punished and our land purified, since they became, as it were, **a ransom for the sin of our nation**. Through the blood of these righteous ones and through **the atonement of their death** the divine providence saved Israel, which had been shamefully treated.* 4 MACCABEES 17 v 20-22, *emphasis mine*

It turns out that a well-schooled Israelite at the time of Jesus could, indeed, theorise about a righteous human's death *atoning* for the wrongdoing of God's people. The historian who takes all of this evidence into account will have no difficulty in imagining that a devout Galilean Jew like Jesus, who believed himself to be central to the kingdom of God, could also have said that his own death at the hands of the Romans *atoned* for his people, preserving them from the judgment coming on the world.

This interpretation of Jesus' death—which seems to be Jesus' *own* interpretation of his death—resolves a tension we find within his message. Jesus was dramatic in his teaching that the kingdom of God would upend the world and overturn the wicked. That was the typical Jewish view. But he also insisted that the lowly and unworthy from the "east and the west" would enter that kingdom. How does Jesus' preaching about strict divine judgment square with his preaching about divine liberality and love? The answer was given more than a century ago by New Testament scholarship's "Einstein figure", Albert Schweitzer: Jesus believed that safety from the coming catastrophe could be found *in himself*, and, in particular, in his death on behalf of others. Here's how Schweitzer put it:

> *In leaving Galilee He abandoned the hope that the final tribulation would begin in itself. If it delays, that means that there is still something to be done ... The time of trial was not come; therefore God in His mercy and omnipotence had eliminated it from the series of eschatological events, and appointed Him whose commission had been to bring it about, instead to accomplish it in His own person. As He who was to rule over the members of the Kingdom in the future age, He was appointed to serve them in the present, to give His life for them, the many, and to make in His own blood the atonement which they would have had to render in the tribulation.*[12]

As I have already said, I am less pessimistic than Schweitzer about whether a genuinely historical understanding of Jesus—and of Jesus' death, in particular—leaves him as an "enigma". After all, it does not require much imagination to see how Jesus' own thinking about his death could inspire the more traditional, more familiar, framing of the crucifixion found in contemporary Christian preaching: "Jesus died for our sins", "He suffered for our forgiveness", and so on.

In the next chapter I will offer further reasons why we can read the life (and death) of Jesus as a genuine histori-

---

12 Albert Schweitzer, *The Quest of the Historical Jesus*. (Dover, 2005), p 387.

cal event, much like the events of other well known figures, such as Alexander the Great.

In A Nutshell

As an initial judgement, we can say with some confidence that central elements of the story the Gospels tell about Jesus fit credibly with what we know of the life and thought of first-century Galilee and Judaea. We can easily envisage a prophet-like figure wandering throughout Israel with a message about "the kingdom of God" and challenging his compatriots *not* to imagine that the kingdom will come through violent freedom-fighting. We can picture him engaged in debates about the precise definition of "work" on the Sabbath, and we can plausibly place him on the liberal end of the spectrum on such matters. And, despite the strangeness (to us) of anyone imagining their own death might atone for the sins of others, the historical record makes plain that the words "this is my blood poured out for you" are both well-attested and highly conceivable in Jesus' period.

Readings

Jesus argues about certain Jewish traditions

The Pharisees and some of the teachers of the law who had come from Jerusalem gathered around

Jesus and saw some of his disciples eating food with hands that were defiled, that is, unwashed...

So the Pharisees and teachers of the law asked Jesus, "Why don't your disciples live according to the tradition of the elders instead of eating their food with defiled hands?" He replied, "Isaiah was right when he prophesied about you hypocrites; as it is written: 'These people honour me with their lips, but their hearts are far from me. They worship me in vain; their teachings are merely human rules.' You have let go of the commands of God and are holding on to human traditions..."

Again Jesus called the crowd to him and said, "Listen to me, everyone, and understand this. Nothing outside a person can defile them by going into them. Rather, it is what comes out of a person that defiles them..."

He went on: "What comes out of a person is what defiles them. For it is from within, out of a person's heart, that evil thoughts come—sexual immorality, theft, murder, adultery, greed, malice, deceit, lewdness, envy, slander, arrogance and folly. All these evils come from inside and defile a person."

MARK 7 v 1-23 (excerpts)

The crucifixion, as recounted in the Gospel of Luke

Two other men, both criminals, were also led out with him to be executed. When they came to the place called the Skull, they crucified him there, along with the criminals—one on his right, the other on his left. Jesus said, "Father, forgive them, for they do not know what they are doing". And they divided up his clothes by casting lots. The people stood watching, and the rulers even sneered at him. They said, "He saved others; let him save himself if he is God's Messiah, the Chosen One." The soldiers also came up and mocked him. They offered him wine vinegar and said, "If you are the king of the Jews, save yourself." There was a written notice above him, which read: THIS IS THE KING OF THE JEWS.

One of the criminals who hung there hurled insults at him: "Aren't you the Messiah? Save yourself and us!" But the other criminal rebuked him. "Don't you fear God," he said, "since you are under the same sentence? We are punished justly, for we are getting what our deeds deserve. But this man has done nothing wrong." Then he said, "Jesus, remember me when you come into your kingdom." Jesus answered him, "Truly I tell you, today you will be with me in paradise."

It was now about noon, and darkness came over the whole land until three in the afternoon, for the sun stopped shining. And the curtain of the temple was torn in two. Jesus called out with a loud voice, "Father, into your hands I commit my spirit." When he had said this, he breathed his last. The centurion, seeing what had happened, praised God and said, "Surely this was a righteous man."

When all the people who had gathered to witness this sight saw what took place, they beat their breasts and went away. But all those who knew him, including the women who had followed him from Galilee, stood at a distance, watching these things.

LUKE 23 v 32-49

The death of Jesus, in a letter of the apostle John

That which was from the beginning, which we have heard, which we have seen with our eyes, which we have looked at and our hands have touched—this we proclaim concerning the Word of life. The life appeared; we have seen it and testify to it, and we proclaim to you the eternal life, which was with the Father and has appeared to us...

This is the message we have heard from him and declare to you: God is light; in him there is no darkness at all. If we claim to have fellowship with him and yet walk in the darkness, we lie and do not live out the truth. But if we walk in the light, as he is in the light, we have fellowship with one another, and the blood of Jesus, his Son, purifies us from all sin.

If we claim to be without sin, we deceive ourselves and the truth is not in us. If we confess our sins, he is faithful and just and will forgive us our sins and purify us from all unrighteousness. If we claim we have not sinned, we make him out to be a liar and his word is not in us.

My dear children, I write this to you so that you will not sin. But if anybody does sin, we have an advocate with the Father—Jesus Christ, the Righteous One. He is the atoning sacrifice for our sins, and not only for ours but also for the sins of the whole world. 1 JOHN 1 V 1 – 2 V 2

What Alexander the Great can teach us about history

So far in this book I have made all sorts of comments about Jesus, Tiberius, Livia, Alexander the Great, Pliny (Elder and Younger) and numerous others. But there is an obvious set of questions: What are the writings that give us "knowledge" about these people? When were they composed? How do we know the texts have not been altered? And what tests do historians apply to such ancient testimony to detect falsehood?

Such questions are asked of *all* historical figures. So, as we explore the material about Jesus, I want to highlight a few methodological parallels between investigating his life and investigating the life of another grand historical figure.

THE GREATEST ALEXANDER

Few names from ancient times are more recognisable than Alexander the Great. We call him "the Great" to distinguish him from fifteen other important but not-quite-so-great "Alexanders" between 500 BC and AD 600. They all get biographical entries in the *Oxford Classical Dictionary*, the one-volume compendium of all things Greek and Roman, mentioned in chapter 3. But *Alexander #3* gets a longer entry than all the other Alexanders put together.

Alexander the Great (356-323 BC) was the son of the Macedonian monarchs Philip I and Olympias. As crown prince, Alexander received the royal treatment, enjoying every imaginable opportunity for advancement, including having a private teacher named Aristotle—yes, *the* Aristotle. That would be like having Bill Gates or Steve Jobs as your tech instructor, or Albert Einstein as your maths tutor.

THE LONG MARCH EAST

In early 334 BC at the age of 22, Alexander set off on what would become an almost non-stop decade-long military campaign eastwards from Greece. His 43,000 foot soldiers and more than 5,000-strong cavalry launched a reign of terror that rarely met with equal resistance. He took Asia Minor (Turkey) within months, and routed the mighty Persians the following year. By 330 BC he was the master of Greece, Asia Minor, Syria, Israel, Egypt and Mesopotamia down to the Persian Gulf. At age 26, I was starting my PhD and having my first child in the suburbs—Alexander was busy ruling the world!

But Alexander was not satisfied. He continued east to see what else he could find to conquer. Amid unbelievably difficult conditions and the occasional mini-rebellion from his own troops—always mercilessly crushed—Alexander crossed the Indus River in 326 BC and defeated the elephant-led armies of the north Indian prince Porus. The next year he returned west as far as Susa, just north of the head of the Persian Gulf, where he enjoyed what you might call a sabbatical (325-324 BC)—he rested from campaigning, married off his nobles to elite Persian women, and developed grandiose plans to expand and consolidate his vast domain. Throughout this period he believed he could conquer anything, and he began to make pretensions to divinity, requiring people to bow before him in the style associated more with gods than rulers.

Fresh military and colonisation projects resumed in 324-323 BC, but Alexander soon contracted an illness—perhaps from an old chest wound, perhaps by poisoning—and after ten days he died on 10th June 323 BC at just 32 years of age.

It is almost impossible to calculate the lasting influence of Alexander's ten-year conquest. He passed through history in a brief blaze of glory, but his deputies divided the conquered territory among themselves and established Greek-style kingdoms all across the Mediterranean and Near East for the next couple of centuries—until the Romans rose to dominance (traditionally dated to 146 BC, the Battle of Corinth). This meant that Greek language, culture, philosophy, and science were disseminated east and west in ways that can still be detected today. We are all, in part, influenced by ancient Greek modes of thought and conduct, and that is mostly a good thing.

HOW WE KNOW WHAT WE KNOW

But how do we know any of the things that I just narrated about Alexander the Great—which you will find in any decent book about him?

Some of our information comes from a few random inscriptions and from the large number of coins of the period. These tell us something about the extent of Alexander's reign, the titles he enjoyed, and his broad dates. But the bulk of what we hold to be true about Alexander comes not from artefacts like these but from written sources composed after Alexander's death and faithfully copied over the centuries in manuscripts now stored in the world's great museums and libraries. Almost everything we know about ancient history, including about Alexander, we know from written testimony composed decades after the fact and preserved in manuscript copies.

Within a generation of Alexander's death, numerous officials composed accounts of his whirlwind career. These include Callisthenes, Nearchus, Ptolemy I and Aristobulus. Unfortunately, none of these accounts have survived. We know of them only because much later writers incorporated these earlier sources into their works.

Probably the best of these later works is that of Lucius Flavius Arrianus, or Arrian (AD 86-160), a philosopher, distinguished writer and friend of Emperor Hadrian (AD 76-138). His work is called the *Anabasis* [meaning "expedition" or "ascent"] *of Alexander*. Arrian wrote it in the early 2nd century AD, and it survives today—after centuries of fairly stable copying—in 36 manuscripts, all of which are copies of a single manuscript known as the Codex Vindobonensis, dated to around the year 1200 and stored in the National Library of Vienna.

Arrian wrote his account of Alexander 400 years after the fact. That may sound *too late* to be of any use, but there are good reasons why historians today regard this work as the best biographical source for Alexander's life. First, throughout his work Arrian draws heavily on the earlier sources mentioned above (particularly Ptolemy and Aristobulus). These sources are lost to us, but they were readily available to Arrian.

If we were in a doubting mood, of course, we could easily argue that Arrian made everything up—that he pretended to have earlier sources in front of him and simply invented everything he claimed came from his sources. But that would be arbitrary scepticism. Using earlier sources within historical works was the norm in this period (as today). We would need a good reason to suspect "invention" before we travelled too far down such a distrusting path.

Arrian's tone is also relatively *fair-minded*. While he is prone to defending the memory of Alexander—excusing his excesses, for example, by saying he was merely a youthful hothead—he is nonetheless quite capable of questioning his own sources and leaving some claims about Alexander open for his readers to judge. Here is a brief taste of Arrian's style from the opening lines of his work:

> *Wherever Ptolemy son of Lagus and Aristobulus son of Aristobulus have both given the same accounts of Alexander son of Philip, it is my practice to record what they say as completely true, but where they differ, to select the version I regard as more trustworthy and also better worth telling. In fact other writers have given a variety of accounts of Alexander, nor is there any other figure of whom there are more historians who are more contradictory of each other, but in my view Ptolemy and Aristobulus are more trustworthy in their narrative…*
>
> ANABASIS OF ALEXANDER 1.1-3

Arrian comes across as a "fan" of Alexander, for sure, but one who is nonetheless informed and level-headed. This sort of thing matters to contemporary historians reading Arrian's material. Just as a judge in a court of law often makes private notes during testimony about the believability of various witnesses, so historians today pay attention to the tone and measure of historical sources and make judgements about credibility. As a result, experts in Greek history tend to rank Arrian as the chief ancient witness to the career of Alexander the Great.

The key Greek-English edition of the *Anabasis of Alexandria* introduces us to the work with the firm judgement, "Arrian unquestionably provides us with the best evidence we have for Alexander."[13]

No one accepts everything Arrian says about Alexander the Great. The broad plausibility of the story has to be checked against all that is known of the archaeology, writings, culture, and politics of Greece, Israel, Egypt, Persia, and even India, in the fourth century BC. Specific claims are double checked against other accounts of Alexander, whether the passing comments in Polybius (200-118 BC) and Strabo (63 BC – AD 23) or the stylised biography written by Plutarch (AD 46-120). Rarely will today's specialists fret about trying to verify specific details of things said by Alexander (or his generals), but they will certainly pay attention to the general character and recurring motifs of his conquests, methods, and ambitions. As a result, there is wide agreement today about the general course of Alexander's career, the sorts of things he said and did, and the impact he made on the Mediterranean and ancient Near East.

THE GREATEST JESUS

But what does any of this have to do with Jesus of Nazareth? There were many people named "Jesus" in the ancient world. Based on an academic database of over 500 different ancient Jewish names, we can calculate that "Jesus"— or *Yeshua*—was the sixth most popular male name in the period.

---

13 Arrian. *Anabasis of Alexander, Volume I: Books 1-4*, translated by P. A. Brunt, Loeb Classical Library 236. (Harvard University Press, 1976), p xvi.

Quite a few men named Jesus appear across our historical records. Even in the New Testament there are a couple of *other* people named Jesus. For example, the apostle Paul mentions one in passing as he sends greetings to the church in Colossae (in southwest Turkey) from various missionary colleagues: "Jesus, who is called Justus, sends greetings" (Colossians 4 v 11). Perhaps this man felt awkward about sharing a name with his Lord, so after becoming a Christian he asked to be called Justus, which pretty much rhymes with Jesus in the original Greek.

Today, one "Jesus" eclipses all others. In long historical perspective, the man from Nazareth is not just *the greatest "Jesus"*; he is arguably the most recognisable name from *all* of ancient history—more than Cleopatra, more than Julius, and even more than the *great* Alexander.

UNFAIR COMPARISON?

Comparing Alexander the Great and Jesus of Nazareth is precarious. Not only were their career paths and leadership styles radically different but Alexander was, it must be said, infinitely more influential in his day than Jesus was in his. The former was a tornado that swept across the world from Greece to India. The latter was a blip on the radar of Galilee and Judaea—backwaters of the Roman Empire. We should not be fooled by the fact that Jesus founded *what would become* the world's largest religion. In his day, he was merely a big fish in the small pond of Galilee.

What this means is that we should not expect the historical evidence for Jesus to be equal to that for Alexander. No one in antiquity would have thought to mint coins for a Jewish rabbi. It would not have entered anyone's mind to create an inscription on stone for an itinerant preacher (and martyr) who never "campaigned" further than the rough distance of Sydney to Newcastle, London to Cambridge, or New York to Philadelphia.

Even Socrates, Greece's most revered teacher and also a martyr, never earned himself a coin or an inscription. Yet, viewed from another angle, while the quality and quantity of evidence for Alexander and Jesus will naturally be different, the historical principles for studying the figures are the same. And in some important respects our evidence for Jesus is superior to that of Alexander.

DATE OF WRITING

Leaving aside inscriptions and coins, the earliest biographical information we have for Alexander is the remarks of Polybius, writing 120 years after Alexander's death; and our *best* source, as I have said, was written by Arrian 400 years after the king's death.

What about our sources for Jesus? The Gospels offer our best biographical information about Jesus. The commonly accepted dates for these first-century works are the 60s for Mark, the 70s-80s for Luke and Matthew, and the 90s for the Gospel of John. In other words, we have a full biography of Jesus within 40 years of his death, another two within 50 years, and a fourth within 70 years. Put baldly, the latest existing biographical source for Jesus (John's Gospel) is closer in time to its subject than is the earliest existing biographical source for Alexander (Polybius).

If we compare our *best* sources for the two figures, the comparison is even more interesting. Mark and Luke are generally considered to be of most historical worth for the study of Jesus (Christians see all of the Bible as the Word of God and equally valuable; historians do not). These books were written between 30 and 50 years after Jesus' death. Arrian was written 400 years after Alexander.

Perhaps a fairer comparison is with the emperor of Jesus' day: Tiberius (AD 14-37). Leaving aside inscriptions and coins, the pre-eminent source for our knowledge of Tiberius is the account of a Roman aristocrat and government official named Cornelius Tacitus, whose *Annals* provide a wealth of information about several emperors of this period.

Tacitius wrote the *Annals* around AD 115-118. That is about 80 years after Tiberius' death. Given that Jesus and Tiberius lived at roughly the same time, the comparison is valuable. The *latest* of the sources used to study Jesus (John's Gospel) was written 20 years earlier than Tacitus' account of the man who ruled the world at the same time as Jesus. And we have sources for Jesus from much earlier than that. Of course, the date of a writing is not the only factor in determining historical worth—as Arrian's account of Alexander makes clear—but it is at least worth remembering that a time gap of 20-70 years between an ancient figure and numerous biographical writings about him or her is pretty good.

SOURCES WITHIN SOURCES

Another historical comparison between the writings about Alexander (and Tiberius) and those about Jesus is *the use of sources*. I previously explained that Arrian incorporated into his *Anabasis of Alexander* the much earlier material of Ptolemy and Aristobulus, who wrote in the decades immediately after Alexander. Sadly, those writings are now lost to us, but they were available to Arrian, and in his opening paragraphs (quoted earlier) he alerts us to the fact that he studied and used sources from the first generation after Alexander. The same is true of the biographies about Jesus.

It is well known that the Gospel-writers employed earlier sources within their works. They themselves wrote 40-70 years after Jesus, but they happily consulted much earlier material and incorporated it into their work. The opening paragraph of the Gospel of Luke (written in the 70s of the first century) alludes to previous writings and to his study of all the relevant material:

> *Many have undertaken to draw up an account of the things that have been fulfilled among us, just as they were handed down to us by those who from the first were eyewitnesses and servants of the word. With this in mind, since I myself have carefully investigated everything from the beginning, I too decided to write an orderly account for you, most excellent Theophilus, so that you may know the certainty of the things you have been taught.* LUKE 1 v 1-4

Today's scholars are intrigued by Luke's reference to "many" written accounts about Jesus. Luke himself was not an eyewitness. He was a follower of Christ within about 15 years of Jesus' death. He became a missionary assistant to the apostle Paul in the late 40s and was acquainted with several eyewitnesses of Jesus in the 50s (if not before), including James the brother of Jesus. Luke wrote his Gospel a decade or so after these heady days, but it is still fascinating that already by the 70s "many" others had done what Luke was setting out to do: "draw up an account" of the things that "eyewitnesses" handed down.

Most contemporary experts believe they can detect three earlier sources within Luke's Gospel:

1. The Gospel of Mark written in the 60s.

2. A collection of Jesus' teachings known as "Q" (from the German *die Quelle* or "the source") dating to the 40s or 50s.

3. A collection of parables, stories and sayings dubbed simply "L" (meaning Luke's unique source) from the 50s.

Although two of these sources are now lost to us (Q and L), they were known to Luke and were incorporated into his work, in a manner not unlike Arrian's use of the now-lost Ptolemy and Aristobulus manuscripts.

TESTING LUKE

One obvious difference between Arrian's use of Ptolemy and Aristobulus and Luke's use of Mark, Q, and L is that Arrian often says things like "Ptolemy reports [such and such]". Luke never does that. Luke is more like Tacitus, who also used earlier sources for his account of Emperor Tiberius but never explicitly cited them in the way Arrian did.

On the other hand, Luke's Gospel allows us to do something important that we cannot do with many other ancient writings. We can *test* how faithful Luke was to his earlier sources.

Luke would never have imagined that centuries after he wrote his Gospel, scholars would develop a historical sub-discipline known as source analysis or redaction criticism, where experts keenly double-check the way a writer (whether Arrian, Tacitus or Luke) uses the source material in their works.

For example, we can take a copy of the Gospel of Mark (one of sources Luke used) and compare it with Luke's *use* of Mark in the Gospel of Luke. About a third of Luke's material comes straight from Mark (the remainder comes from Q, L, and Luke's own editorial work). When we compare Mark's Gospel with Luke's *use* of Mark's Gospel, it becomes clear that Luke was faithful to his earlier source, even though he never could have imagined that we would check up on him. At the end of this chapter—in the "Readings" section—I offer a portion of the Gospel of Mark set alongside Luke's use of that portion of Mark as a source. Readers can see for themselves Luke's tendency to *conserve* rather than *innovate*.

MANUSCRIPT COPIES

There is another way in which our brief study of Alexander the Great provides something of a parallel for understanding how historians study Jesus. I noted earlier that we have 36 manuscript copies of Arrian's *Anabasis of Alexander*, all of which depend on a single manuscript of the work copied out around the year 1200.

Given what we know of the care ancient and medieval scribes took in copying out such precious volumes, no one really doubts that the *Anabasis* we read today is pretty much as Arrian wrote it a thousand or so years earlier.

How many manuscript copies of the Gospels do we possess today? And how confident can we be that ancient and medieval copyists have preserved what was written down in the first century? This is one of the areas where all scholars agree that the material concerning Jesus eclipses everything else from the period.

It is no exaggeration to say that the writings about Jesus are—with the exception of inscriptions written in stone—the best-attested records from all classical history. Even as sharp a critic of Christian beliefs as Bart Ehrman has acknowledged that...

Textual scholars have enjoyed reasonable success at establishing, to the best of their abilities, the original text of the New Testament.[14]

The reason for our confidence in the text of the New Testament is *not* that Christians were so brilliant at the copying task (some of them were really quite clumsy). It is the sheer number of ancient and medieval manuscripts in our possession that makes the difference. As Stanley Porter, a leader in the field, remarks in his entry on "Manuscripts" in *A Dictionary of the New Testament Background...* [15]

There are approximately fifty-five hundred manuscripts [yes, that's 5,500] of the Greek New Testament, depending upon how they are counted. The number is larger than for any other ancient Greek or Latin author or book."

Many of these manuscripts are small fragments—perhaps half a chapter of a single Gospel—but even such fragments help us confirm sections of the more complete manuscripts.

In the Sackler Library Papyrology Rooms in Oxford, I recently got to handle the oldest known fragment of the Gospel of Mark. Only six verses—scattered across Mark 1— are legible, but the wording compares almost precisely with our other manuscripts of Mark.

The important thing is the vast number. The greater the number of manuscripts, the easier it is to detect a "variant" or mistake in one of the copies. Imagine you had in your possession just three copies of an important handwritten letter, and one of the copies differed in several paragraphs

---

14 Bart Ehrman and Michael Holmes, *The Text of the New Testament in Contemporary Research.* (Eerdmans, 1995), p 375.

15 p 670.

from the others. With so few copies, it would be difficult to know which wording was *original* and which was an *alteration*. But imagine you had hundreds of copies of the same letter. In that case, the task of spotting errors and judging what was original is much, much easier.

ANOTHER COMPARISON

Perhaps it *is* unfair to compare the text of the New Testament with the text of Arrian's *Anabasis of Alexander*. The truth is, it is unfair to compare the New Testament with any ancient document.

But let me offer a closer parallel. One of the most plentifully preserved texts of Roman history is Virgil's *Aeneid*, an epic poem in twelve books written just 50 years before Jesus. It tells the rollicking tale of the hero Aeneas, who survived the battle of Troy, fell in love with the dangerous Dido, and eventually settled in Italy, where he founded the city of Rome. The work is preserved today in three (virtually) complete manuscripts, seven very large partial manuscripts (each containing many pages of the work), and twenty fragments (often just a page). This is among the best-attested texts of ancient Rome.

The New Testament is preserved today in four (virtually) complete manuscripts. This compares nicely to the *Aeneid*. But we also have over 300 large partial manuscripts—keep in mind, a large partial manuscript might contain three of the four Gospels, or eight of Paul's letters. And, of course, the number of fragments (single pages or portions of pages) is literally in the thousands.

Not only is the *number* of manuscript copies significant; so is the *date* they were copied. The oldest manuscript of Arrian's *Anabasis* is from about AD 1200, as I have said. All of the manuscripts of Virgil's *Aeneid* date from the 4th to the 9th centuries. The New Testament manuscripts are earlier, with most of them coming from the 4th to the 6th centuries, and some from the 2nd and 3rd centuries.

For example, stored in a climate-controlled vault in the Chester Beatty Library in Dublin is a wonderful copy of several of Paul's letters in a manuscript dated to AD 200. It is called simply *Papyrus 46*. I got to hold one of its pages some years ago for a documentary on the sources of our knowledge of Jesus. I was overawed and stupidly asked the curator how much it was worth. He looked down his nose at me—the colonial boy—and insisted, "We do not discuss such things!" Fair enough.

There are also copies of the Gospels from around the same time (*Papyrus 45, Papyrus 64, Papyrus 76*—none of which I have yet got to handle). These manuscripts are *a couple of centuries older* than our best manuscript of the *Aeneid*, and *a thousand years older* than our best manuscript of Arrian's *Anabasis*.

It is a quirk of history—Christians might say divine providence—that a man from Nazareth, who in his day had nothing of the impact of people like Alexander, Tiberius, or even Virgil, is documented in texts which,

1. were composed relatively close in time to the events they record;

2. faithfully incorporate even earlier sources; and

3. were copied far more widely than any other work from the same period.

None of this *proves* the story of Jesus—this is not that sort of book. But it does go some way to explaining why the accounts of Jesus' life remain the subject of serious historical investigation today.

In A Nutshell

At least three aspects of ancient written sources are of great interest to today's scholars, whether they are studying Alexander the Great or Jesus of Nazareth: What is the date of the writing? What earlier sources are employed in the writing? And how well-preserved are the manuscript copies of the writing? On all three tests, the Gospels and letters of Paul now in the New Testament compare—to put it mildly—well.

Readings

Alexander's defeat of the elephant armies of Porus in India, as told by Arrian

The Indians lost nearly 20,000 foot soldiers, and up to 3,000 horsemen; all the chariots were broken to pieces; two sons of Porus perished, the commanders of the elephants and the cavalry and the generals of Porus' army to a man. And all the surviving elephants were captured. Alexander's army lost about 80 foot soldiers at most out of the force, which had been 6,000 strong in the first attack; as for the cavalry, ten of the mounted archers, who were the first to engage, and about 20 of the Companions' cavalry with 200 other troopers were killed. Porus had acquitted himself manfully in the battle not only as a commander-in-chief but also as a brave soldier …

Unlike the great King Darius, he still did not

set his own men an example of flight, but battled on, so long as any part of the Indian troops held their ground in the fight as an organised unit; only when wounded on the right shoulder did he too at last wheel his elephant round and retreat ... Then Alexander spoke to him first and urged him to say what he desired to be done with him. Porus is said to have replied: "Treat me, Alexander, like a king," and Alexander, pleased with the reply, answered: "That you shall have, Porus, for my own sake; now demand what you would wish for yours." He replied that everything was comprised in this one request. Alexander was the more pleased with this reply, and gave Porus the government of his Indians and added still further territory even greater in extent to his old realm.   ANABASIS OF ALEXANDER 5.18-19

A portion of the Gospel of Mark set alongside Luke's use of that portion

Mark 1 v 21-39

[A scene in the synagogue]
They went to Capernaum, and when the Sabbath came, Jesus went into the synagogue and began to teach. The people were amazed at his teaching, because he taught them as one who had authority, not as the teachers of the law. Just then a man in their synagogue who was possessed by an impure spirit cried out, "What do you want with us, Jesus of

Luke 4 v 31-44

[A scene in the synagogue]
Then he went down to Capernaum, a town in Galilee, and on the Sabbath he taught the people. They were amazed at his teaching, because his words had authority.

In the synagogue there was a man possessed by a demon, an impure spirit. He cried out at the top of his voice, "Go away! What do you want with us, Jesus of

Nazareth? Have you come to destroy us? I know who you are—the Holy One of God!"

"Be quiet!" said Jesus sternly. "Come out of him!" The impure spirit shook the man violently and came out of him with a shriek.

The people were all so amazed that they asked each other, "What is this? A new teaching – and with authority! He even gives orders to impure spirits and they obey him." News about him spread quickly over the whole region of Galilee.

[Various healings]

As soon as they left the synagogue, they went with James and John to the home of Simon and Andrew. Simon's mother-in-law was in bed with a fever, and they immediately told Jesus about her. So he went to her, took her hand and helped her up. The fever left her and she began to wait on them.

That evening after sunset the people brought to Jesus all who were ill and demon-possessed. The whole town gathered at the door, and Jesus healed many who had various diseases. He also drove out many demons, but he would not let the demons speak because they knew who he was.

Nazareth? Have you come to destroy us? I know who you are—the Holy One of God!"

"Be quiet!" Jesus said sternly. "Come out of him!" Then the demon threw the man down before them all and came out without injuring him.

All the people were amazed and said to each other, "What words these are! With authority and power he gives orders to impure spirits and they come out!" And the news about him spread throughout the surrounding area.

[Various healings]

Jesus left the synagogue and went to the home of Simon. Now Simon's mother-in-law was suffering from a high fever, and they asked Jesus to help her. So he bent over her and rebuked the fever, and it left her. She got up at once and began to wait on them.

At sunset, the people brought to Jesus all who had various kinds of illness, and laying his hands on each one, he healed them. Moreover, demons came out of many people, shouting, "You are the Son of God!" But he rebuked them and would not allow them to speak, because they knew he was the Messiah.

Scraps about Jesus

There are several passing references to Jesus within a century of his death in the writings of people who were not Christians. Admittedly, they are mere "scraps". But these texts attract a lot of attention, especially on the internet, although they are not nearly as significant as Christians might hope, nor as flimsy as sceptical folk imagine.

People are interested in such extra-biblical writings because they see them as *objective* evidence for Jesus, whereas the New Testament is seen as *subjective* and tainted. That is not how specialists see the matter.

Textual bias

There is no theoretical difference between Christian and non-Christian references to Jesus. From the historical point of view, they are both just *human* texts which must be assessed on *historical* grounds rather than religious, or irreligious, grounds. The Christian writings—the Gospels and Paul's letters mainly—are important not because they deserve to be privileged as "sacred" but because they are early, employ even earlier sources, and give a much fuller—and therefore more easily testable—account of Jesus' life.

Their Christian perspective (or bias) is no more a black mark against them than a Roman perspective (or bias) makes Tacitus an untrustworthy writer about the emperors. Similarly, the non-Christian references to Jesus explored below are not given extra credit for *not being Christian* (just as the New Testament does not lose credit for *being Christian*). They are assessed for what they are: human texts written within a century of Jesus. The limited value of the non-biblical references to Jesus discussed below is a consequence of their relative late date (compared to the New Testament), their brevity, and their lack of interest or care about the subject.

Still, in my classes at Sydney University on this subject we give three hours to all eleven scraps of non-Christian information about Jesus. It is usually more fun than it sounds. What follows is the nutshell version, focusing on just the two most significant sources: one Roman, the other Jewish.

CORNELIUS TACITUS

Much of what we learned at school about the Roman emperors Augustus, Tiberius, Caligula, Claudius and Nero comes directly from the works of Cornelius Tacitus. He is a central source of our information about this imperial period, which is why I have mentioned him so often already in this book.

Tacitus was born around AD 56. He was an aristocrat who rose up through the ranks of Roman society and politics before becoming Rome's head man or proconsul in the province of "Asia", what is now Turkey. He wrote a biography of his father-in-law, Agricola, an important Roman general, and a history of the emperors that reigned between AD 69 and 96—most of which is sadly now lost. His most important work, for our purposes, is his *Annals*, which recounts the careers of the Emperors Tiberius (AD 14-37), Caligula (37-41), Claudius (41-54) and Nero (54-69). With a first-class education and unfettered access to imperial sources, Tacitus was uniquely placed to write such a history.

The *Annals* survives today in just two partial manuscripts—one copied in the 9th century (covering the first half of the work) and another copied in the 11th century (covering the second half of the work). Both are stored in the beautiful Laurentian Library in Florence. The occasional internet article—keen to debunk Christianity—will claim that these manuscripts are forgeries, in part or in whole, but that is not the view taught in any university classics or ancient history department today.

CHRISTIANS AND THE FIRE OF ROME

Tacitus mentions Jesus only briefly and only in passing. He is not at all interested in Jesus. He mentions him simply to clarify the origin of the "Christians". The reason he mentions Christians is that Emperor Nero blamed them for the great fire of Rome, which destroyed several of the capital's suburbs over a ten-day period in June AD 64.

Rumours soon circulated that Nero himself had started the fire because he wanted to refurbish parts of the city. Whether or not the emperor was behind it (he was 50km away at his villa in Antium when the fire broke out), it suited him to blame this new group of religious upstarts called the Christians—everyone, it seemed, already hated them. Here is Tacitus' account:

> *Therefore, to scotch the rumour, Nero substituted as culprits, and punished with the utmost refinements of cruelty, a class of men, loathed for their vices, whom*

the crowd styled Christians. Christus, the founder of the name, had undergone the death penalty in the reign of Tiberius, by sentence of the procurator Pontius Pilatus, and the pernicious superstition was checked for a moment, only to break out once more, not merely in Judaea, the home of the disease, but in the capital itself, where all things horrible or shameful in the world collect and find a vogue. First, then, the confessed members of the sect were arrested; next, on their disclosures, vast numbers were convicted, not so much on the count of arson as for hatred of the human race. And derision accompanied their end: they were covered with wild beasts' skins and torn to death by dogs; or they were fastened on crosses, and, when daylight failed were burned to serve as lamps by night. Nero had offered his Gardens for the spectacle, and gave an exhibition in his Circus [a games arena], mixing with the crowd in the habit [clothes] of a charioteer. [16]

I have taught about this event for years. It is a poignant reminder that some early Christians—by no means all—endured the most horrendous consequences for their faith. In late 2017, I visited for the first time the spot where Nero's circus once stood. Ironically, or perhaps poetically, it now sits within the walled precincts of Vatican City. I let my imagination run wild, as I pictured scores (probably hundreds) of first-century Roman believers rounded up, brought to this public arena and slaughtered in front of the crowds for entertainment. I wondered how they could have maintained Jesus' famous command: "Love your enemies. Do good to those who hate you." I wondered if I could have endured what they did.

---

16   Tacitus, *Annals* 15.44. The translation is that of John Jackson, *Loeb Classical Library* vol.322. (Harvard University Press, 1999)

Tacitus was obviously no fan of this "pernicious superstition", but he manages to offer a few pieces of good information about Jesus. The passage is excellent evidence of the elite Roman hatred of Christians, in both the time of Nero and the time of Tacitus. But the passing clarification about the execution of the Jew "Christus" provides obvious corroboration for Jesus' death in Judaea during the governorship of Pontius Pilate (AD 26-36).

ERRORS

It is worth pointing out that Tacitus makes two minor errors in this passage. He wrongly assumes that "Christus" is a personal name, rather than a title ("Christ" or "Messiah"). And he gives Pontius Pilate the wrong title.

Pilate was commissioned not as "procurator" but as *prefect* or governor, as a stone inscription found in Caesarea Maritima on the coast of Israel confirms. This illustrates something I have stressed throughout the book. Historical sources tend to be good at providing broadly reliable accounts of ancient events and people, but we are right to be cautious about the finer details. No one reads Tacitus' mistakes and declares everything he wrote to be bogus. Historians happily stand back—without pernickety scepticism—and take in the whole view.

In this case, we can confidently say that a Roman official writing well within a century of Jesus, and without any particular interest in Jesus, locates him in the right time and place, and attests to his execution by the correct official. It is not much. But it is something.

FLAVIUS JOSEPHUS

I have mentioned Josephus a few times already in this book. He is the most important source of Jewish history for the first century. Flavius Josephus (37-100) commanded Jewish troops in Galilee in the great war with Rome (66-70), which ended with the sacking of Jerusalem and its magnificent temple. He was priestly, aristocratic, highly educated and brilliant. He left us an autobiography in which he tells us how brilliant he was!

In addition to writing a history of the Jewish-Roman war, Josephus wrote *Jewish Antiquities*, a twenty-volume account of the Jewish people from "creation" to the outbreak of the war in AD 66. For the early bits, Josephus simply uses his Bible, the Old Testament, restating things in very interesting ways for his Greek and Roman readers. For the later sections—covering the period from about 200 BC to AD 69—he uses a range of sources, most of which are now lost to us.

JESUS THE "WISE MAN"

In Book 18 of the *Antiquities,* while narrating the events of Pontius Pilate's governorship of Judaea, Josephus mentions Jesus in passing. It is a single paragraph, but it has generated a huge amount of discussion, with sceptics trying to argue that it is a forgery and Christian apologists attempting to defend its credibility.

To cut a long story short, the overwhelming judgement of specialists today is that Josephus really did write a short statement about Pilate's execution of Jesus, but that a Christian copiest later tried to "enhance" the passage. Part of the reason scholars have arrived at this consensus is that it is fairly easy to detect *two* hands in the wording of the paragraph: one which is neutral or stand-off-ish, and another that is glowingly Christian. Here is the passage with the "Christian enhancements" in bold:

> *About this time there lived Jesus, a wise man,* **if indeed one ought to call him a man.** *For he was one who wrought surprising feats and was a teacher of such people as accept the truth gladly. He won over many Jews and many of the Greeks.* **He was the Messiah.** *When Pilate, upon hearing him accused by men of the highest standing amongst us, had condemned him to be crucified, those who had in the first place come to love him did not give up their affection for him.* **On the third day he appeared to them restored to life, for the prophets of God had prophesied these and countless other marvellous things about him.** *And the tribe of the Christians, so called after him, has still to this day not disappeared.*
>
> JEWISH ANTIQUITIES 18.63-64, *emphasis mine*

When I read this out to my class each year, I have to resist the temptation to speak in two different voices: one that calmly and disinterestedly describes Jesus simply as "a wise man" and another that *counters* with "if indeed one ought to call him a man"! What seems to have happened is that an originally plain-speaking statement from the Jewish writer has been "improved" in the copying process by some unknown Christian scribe. We do not know how this happened.

It is possible that a sneaky Christian thought they could alter the text to make it more theologically sound without anyone noticing. But it may have happened more innocently. The words in bold above may originally have been comments in the margin made by a scribe who did not want the next reader of the manuscript to be led astray by Josephus' pedestrian view of Jesus. But when the next scribe came to make a copy of Josephus, they were unsure about the status of the marginal remarks and decided to play it safe by incorporating them into their new, clean copy of the work. We will probably never know.

The remarks in bold in the quote above would not have been written by a writer like Josephus, who was not a Christian. We can be confident about that. Equally, several of the other lines are unlikely to have been invented by a Christian. First, as I have just said, the words "a wise man" (*sophos anēr*) present a sub-Christian view of Jesus. It is an expression Josephus uses elsewhere in his works to describe ordinary human beings. It is *not* a description that the church ever used of Jesus. This alone probably explains why a later Christian copyist felt the need to add "if indeed one ought to call him a man".

Second, the words "surprising feats" translate the Greek *paradoxa erga*, literally "unusual/puzzling deeds". It is not a typical way for a Christian to refer to Jesus' healings: the Gospels call such deeds "powers" (*dunameis*) or "signs" (*sēmeia*). The expression makes better sense as a non-Christian's way of referring to Jesus' *reputation* as a healer— whatever Josephus thought might explain that reputation.

Third, those who condemned Jesus are complimentarily described as "men of the highest standing amongst us". This seems unlikely to have come from a Christian hand, since Christians had a rather dim view of those authorities.

Fourth, the statement that Jesus "won over ... many of the Greeks" is flat wrong. Every reader of the New Testament knows that Jesus directed his ministry *to Israel alone* (with a few notable exceptions). We can easily imagine Josephus making such a mistake, since he would not have read the

Gospels or the letters of Paul, but it is unlikely that a Christian scribe would have penned this statement.

Fifth, and finally, it would be odd for a later Christian to say, "the tribe of the Christians has still to this day not disappeared". These words sound as if they come from someone who was surprised that Christians were still around at the end of the first century and who expected them to disappear sometime soon.

NOT IMAGINED

The other important fact sometimes lost in popular discussions is that no one in the ancient or medieval period ever claimed that Jesus did not exist. It would be odd for any ancient or medieval scribe copying out Josephus to feel the need to manufacture "proofs" of Jesus' mere presence in history. We can understand why a scribe might want to "improve" a non-Christian's low view of Jesus, bringing it more into line with what they regarded as good theology, but it is difficult to imagine why they would create such a brief, ambiguous, passing reference to Jesus out of thin air.

None of these lines of reasoning about this passage in *Jewish Antiquities* amount to proof. Historians work more with probabilities and best explanations than proof. And my simple point is that the weight of evidence in this case tips most scholars towards the position described by Graham Stanton of Cambridge:

> *Once the obvious interpolations are removed, this paragraph gives an ambivalent or even mildly hostile assessment of Jesus—one which can be attributed to Josephus with confidence.*[17]

---

17   Graham Stanton, *The Gospels and Jesus*. (Oxford University Press, 2003), p 150.

THE DEATH OF JESUS' BROTHER

Two books later in his work, Josephus mentions Jesus again, and this time there is no hint of scribal embellishment. He mentions the execution of several Jewish men in Jerusalem in the year AD 62. Under the direction of the high priest Ananus, the Sanhedrin, or high court, finds the men guilty of breaking religious law and has them stoned to death. The passage would not grab our attention, except that one of the executed men is described as "James, the brother of Jesus":

> *And so he [Ananus the high priest] convened the judges of the Sanhedrin and brought before them a man named James, the brother of Jesus who was called the Christ, and certain others. He accused them of having transgressed the law and delivered them up to be stoned. Those of the inhabitants of the city who were considered the most fair-minded and who were strict in observance of the law were offended at this.*
>
> JEWISH ANTIQUITIES 20.200

The "James" mentioned here is one of four brothers of Jesus named in the New Testament. Three of these brothers (Joseph, Judas and Simon) became travelling missionaries after Jesus' death (see 1 Corinthians 9 v 5).

The eldest brother, James, stayed in Jerusalem and led the Christian church in the Jewish capital, from the early 30s to the early 60s. This fact is clear from at least two separate, independent sources within the New Testament (Acts 21 v 18; Galatians 1 v 19). But in Josephus we learn something the New Testament doesn't tell us: how James died. James' activities came to the attention of the high priest Ananus, who acted to remove this troublemaker and several other unnamed Christian colleagues. This Ananus was the brother-in-law of the high priest Caiaphas, who had presided over Jesus' trial 30 years earlier. There is probably a story behind this elite family's hatred of Jesus, James and the first Christians, but our sources do not allow us to probe any deeper.

Most interesting for historians is the fact that Josephus identifies James by referring to his better-known brother Jesus, whom, Josephus says, "was called the Christ". It is hard to know whether the original Greek expression—*tou legomenou Christou*—should be translated in a neutral way (as above) or in a more sceptical way: "the so-called Christ". Either way, Josephus does not himself accept Jesus' status as the Messiah. He merely reports the opinion of others.

SIX SCRAPS FROM JOSEPHUS
Josephus leaves us with six small scraps of information:

- the personal name "Jesus" (unlike Tacitus' confusion with "Christus"),
- Jesus' well-known title—"Christ",
- the fact that Jesus had a brother named James,
- the fate of that brother,
- that the Christian movement in Jerusalem remained controversial among the city's leadership for at least 30 years after Jesus,
- and the curious detail that the general population of "fair-minded" folk in Jerusalem objected to the high priest's execution of James and his colleagues.

This last point confirms that the first Jewish Christians in Jerusalem were numerous and/or admired by the general population, something mentioned in passing also in the New Testament (see Acts 2 v 41-47; Acts 4 v 4).

Given that Jesus' existence is not really in any doubt in contemporary scholarship, the remarks of Tacitus and Josephus are of limited significance. Apart from the interesting detail of how and when Jesus' brother James died, there is nothing in these brief passages, these scraps, that *adds* to the historical picture of Jesus we already gleaned from the much *earlier* sources of the Gospels (and the sources within the Gospels) and Paul's letters.

In A Nutshell

Tacitus, the greatest of ancient Rome's chroniclers, mentions Jesus in passing while recounting the events of AD 64 during the reign of Emperor Nero. In one or two sentences, he confirms the title accorded to Jesus (which he confuses with a personal name) and describes him as a criminal duly executed in Judaea while Pontius Pilate governed the region. The Jewish writer Flavius Josephus offers two short paragraphs mentioning Jesus. From these—excluding the lines inserted by a later scribal copiest—we can confirm that the basic facts about Jesus were sufficiently well known in the second half of the first century for a largely disinterested non-Christian author to report them.

Readings

The great fire of Rome (AD 64) according to Tacitus

There followed a disaster, whether due to chance or to the malice of the sovereign is uncertain—for each version has its sponsors—but graver and more terrible than any other which has befallen this city by the ravages of fire ... The flames, which in full career overran the level districts first, then shot up to the heights, and sank again to harry the lower parts, kept ahead of all remedial measures, the mischief travelling fast, and the town being an easy prey owing to the narrow, twisting lanes and formless streets typical of old Rome. In addition, shrieking and terrified women; fugitives stricken or immature in years; men consulting their own safety or the safety of others, as they dragged the infirm along or paused to wait for them, combined by their dilatoriness or their haste to impede everything ...

None ventured to combat the fire, as there were reiterated threats from a large number of persons who forbade extinction, and others were openly throwing firebrands and shouting that "they had their authority"—possibly in order to have a freer hand in looting, possibly from orders received.

Nero, who at the time was staying in Antium did not return to the capital until the fire was nearing the house by which he had connected the Palatine with the Gardens of Maecenas. It proved impossible, however, to stop it from engulfing both the Palatine and the house and all their surroundings. Still, as a relief to the homeless and fugitive populace, he opened the Campus Martius, the buildings of Agrippa, even his own Gardens, and threw up a number of extemporised shelters to accommodate the helpless multitude. The necessities of life were brought up from Ostia and the neighbouring municipalities, and the price of grain was lowered to three sesterces. Yet his measures, popular as their character might be, failed of their effect; for the report had spread that, at the very moment when Rome was aflame, he had mounted his private stage, and, typifying the ills of the present by the calamities of the past, had sung the destruction of Troy.   *Annals* ɪɪ5.38-39

Jesus' brother(s) during his lifetime

Jesus left there and went to his hometown, accompanied by his disciples. When the Sabbath came, he began to teach in the synagogue, and many who heard him were amazed. "Where did this man get these things?" they asked. "What's this wisdom that has been given him? What are these remarkable miracles he is performing? Isn't this the carpenter? Isn't this Mary's son and the brother of James, Joseph, Judas and Simon? Aren't his sisters here with us?" And they took offence at him. Jesus said to them, "A prophet is not without honour except in his own town, among his relatives and in his own home."

MARK 6 v 1-4

After this, Jesus went around in Galilee. He did not want to go about in Judaea because the Jewish leaders there were looking for a way to kill him. But when the Jewish Festival of Tabernacles was near, Jesus' brothers said to him, "Leave Galilee and go to Judaea, so that your disciples there may see the works you do. No one who wants to become a public figure acts in secret. Since you are doing these things, show yourself to the world." For even his own brothers did not believe in him.

JOHN 7 v 1-5

The appearance of Jesus to his brother James

For what I received I passed on to you as of first importance: that Christ died for our sins according to the Scriptures, that he was buried, that he was raised on the third day according to the Scriptures, and that he appeared to Cephas, and then to the Twelve. After that, he appeared to more than five hundred of the brothers and sisters at the same time, most of whom are still living, though some have fallen asleep. Then he appeared to James [the brother of Jesus], then to all the apostles, and last of all he appeared to me also, as to one abnormally born.

Letter of Paul: 1 CORINTHIANS 15 v 3-8

An excerpt from the New Testament letter of James (the brother of Jesus) to the first Jewish Christians

My brothers and sisters, believers in our glorious Lord Jesus Christ must not show favouritism. Suppose a man comes into your meeting wearing a gold ring and fine clothes, and a poor man in filthy old clothes also comes in. If you show special attention to the man wearing fine clothes and say, "Here's a good seat for you," but say to the poor man, "You stand there" or "Sit on the floor by my feet," have you not discriminated among yourselves and become judges with evil thoughts? Listen, my dear brothers and sisters: Has not God chosen those who are poor in the eyes of the world to be rich in faith and to inherit the kingdom he promised those who love him? But you have dishonoured the poor. Is it not the rich who are exploiting you? Are they not the ones who are dragging you into court? Are they not the ones who are blaspheming the noble name of him to whom you belong? If you really keep the royal law found in Scripture, "Love your neighbour as yourself," you are doing right. But if you show favouritism, you sin and are convicted by the law as lawbreakers. JAMES 2 v 1-9

Paul: a Skeleton key to Jesus?

I have frequently been asked, "If Christ really rose again from the dead, why did he appear only to the faithful and not to any sceptics or enemies?" It is a fair question.

But the answer is that he *did* appear to his sceptics and enemies, in at least one case. Leaving aside what we might make of a claim like the resurrection, the fact is that one of the principal writers of the New Testament was *initially* an extremely hostile opponent of Christianity. It's just that when he saw the risen Jesus, he promptly became a disciple.

THE ORIGINAL "DAMASCUS ROAD" EXPERIENCE

Paul, also known as Saul, was a one-time persecutor of the Christians. In about AD 31-32, while on assignment to arrest Christians in Damascus, he encountered the one whose memory he had sought to destroy during the previous year. Here are his own words to Christians in Turkey some years later:

> For you have heard of my previous way of life in Judaism, how intensely I persecuted the church of God and

tried to destroy it. I was advancing in Judaism beyond many of my own age among my people and was extremely zealous for the traditions of my fathers. But when God, who set me apart from birth and called me by his grace, was pleased to reveal his Son in me so that I might preach him among the Gentiles, my immediate response was not to consult any human being. I did not go up to Jerusalem to see those who were apostles before I was, but I went into Arabia. Later I returned to Damascus.

Then after three years, I went up to Jerusalem to get acquainted with Cephas [the apostle Peter] and stayed with him fifteen days. I saw none of the other apostles—only James, the Lord's brother. I assure you before God that what I am writing to you is no lie.

Then I went to Syria and Cilicia. I was personally unknown to the churches of Judea that are in Christ. They only heard the report: "The man who formerly persecuted us is now preaching the faith he once tried to destroy." And they praised God because of me.

GALATIANS 1 v 13-24

Paul does not give many narrative details of his persecution of Christians or of his encounter with Jesus. This is partly because the story was already well known. Even in faraway Turkey people "have heard" the remarkable news of the persecutor turned promoter of the Christian faith.

For the full narrative details of Paul's conversion we rely on the testimony of Luke, the author of the Gospel that bears that name and a sometime travelling companion of Paul. Luke also wrote the New Testament book of Acts, an account of how the message about Jesus was spread around the Mediterranean world in the three decades after Jesus.

Luke penned this history of the early church only about 20 years after Paul's letter to the Galatians quoted above. Yet, as most scholars note, there is little indication that he knew any of Paul's existing letters, let alone this particular one written to Galatia.

In the book of Acts, Luke tells the story of Paul's conversion no fewer than three times. It is clearly important to him. On the first occasion, he narrates it himself as part of his own account of the first year or so of the spread of Christianity out from Jerusalem (Acts 9). The second and third times, Luke relates the conversion story as part of speeches Paul himself gives before a crowd in Jerusalem (Acts 22) and before King Agrippa in Caesarea Maritima (Acts 26).

As scholars observe, all three versions of the story differ slightly. This is interesting. They are plainly the same story, in the work of a single author. But there is enough variation in the accounts for us to conclude that each time Luke recounts the story, he is not glancing back at what he wrote earlier in the scroll and copying it out; he is retelling a well-known story *from memory*. And he is doing it with the same flexibility and fixity we find in a modern long-form joke or in any oft-repeated story we tell—how I met my wife, how I chose my profession, what happened when I crashed the car.

Over the page is a table with the central part of the story in all three version with the similarities in bold, so we can more easily note the differences:

Acts 9 v 3-6	Acts 22 v 6-10	Acts 26 v 12-16
As he **neared Damascus on his journey,** suddenly a light from heaven flashed around him. **He fell to the ground** and **heard a voice** say to him, **"Saul, Saul, why do you persecute me?"** "Who are you, Lord?" Saul asked. **"I am Jesus,** whom **you are persecuting,"** he replied. "Now **get up** and go into the city, and you will be told what you must do."	"About noon as **I came near Damascus,** suddenly a **bright light from heaven** flashed around me. **I fell to the ground** and heard a voice say to me, **'Saul! Saul! Why do you persecute me?'** **'Who are you, Lord?'** I asked. **'I am Jesus of Nazareth,** whom **you are persecuting,'** he replied. My companions saw the light, but they did not understand the voice of him who was speaking to me. 'What shall I do, Lord?' I asked. **'Get up,'** the Lord said, 'and go into Damascus. There you will be told all that you have been assigned to do.'	**"On one of these journeys I was going to Damascus** with the authority and commission of the chief priests. About noon, King Agrippa, as I was on the road, I saw **a light from heaven,** brighter than the sun, blazing around me and my companions. **We all fell to the ground, and I heard a voice** saying to me in Aramaic, **'Saul, Saul, why do you persecute me?** It is hard for you to kick against the goads.' "Then I asked, **'Who are you, Lord?'** **'I am Jesus**, whom **you are persecuting,'** the Lord replied. 16 'Now **get up** and stand on your feet.

James Dunn, an expert on the origins of Christianity from Durham University, makes the point that a lot of historical memory, or "oral tradition", operates in a way that we can observe in this account of Paul's conversion. The broad story (and key particulars) tend to be locked down firmly—a bit like the punchline of a gag or the climactic point of the story of meeting my wife. Yet each retelling will vary depending on the situation. It is not that the 100th retelling is more "evolved" than the fifth retelling; every retelling will display a similar degree of uniformity and variation.[18]

With Paul's own account of his story and the three retellings in the book of Acts, few today doubt that within a year or so of Jesus' crucifixion a Jewish zealot and persecutor of Christianity underwent a radical change: the original "Damascus Road experience".

PAUL THE LETTER-WRITER

From the moment of his conversion until the time of his death three decades later, Paul devoted himself to proclaiming what he once despised. The crucified man Jesus was—so Paul now believed—God's appointed Lord of the world. He was the Messiah, the Son of God.

Paul took this message not only to his fellow Jews but also to non-Jews: "so that I might preach him among the Gentiles," as he put it. He founded communities of believers and stayed in touch with them via letters, answering their questions, settling disputes, and constantly reminding them not to forget the good news or "gospel", he had preached to them.

Only a handful of these letters has survived. They all date from a ten-year period between the early 50s and 60s, after which he was probably martyred in Rome.[19]

---

18 James Dunn, *Jesus Remembered: Christianity in the Making, Volume 1* (Eerdmans, 2003), p 248-49.

19 The historical source for the martyrdom of Paul, by beheading, is Eusebius, *Ecclesiastical History* 2.25.5-6. There is little reason to doubt the account.

At first glance, Paul's letters are not a very exciting source for the history of Jesus. You will search in vain for anything like a *narrative* description of Jesus' birth, teachings, healings, or even the death and resurrection. As a result of this observation, some critics dismiss, or simply overlook, the letters of Paul as sources of information about the history of Jesus. But on closer inspection, Paul's letters turn out to contain first-rate testimony to the earthly Jesus.

Donald Harman Akenson, Professor of History at Queen's University in Canada, has even called Paul's letters a "skeleton key" to understanding the historical Jesus—a kind of master key that unlocks many historical doors. In his fascinating book *Saint Saul: A Skeleton Key to the Historical Jesus*, Akenson made the case that Paul's letters have remarkable proximity to the first years after Jesus' death. As a man personally acquainted with the first disciples, including Jesus' brothers, Paul is about as close to the action as we could hope for in a primary source from antiquity.

The value of Paul's letters, in addition to their early date, lies not in any narration of Jesus' life but in Paul's numerous *passing* references to things Jesus said and did, while discussing various other topics. When talking about marriage, for instance, Paul recalls what Christ said about marital fidelity. When rebuking the rich for their drunken feasts, he reminds readers of the sober significance of Jesus' Last Supper. When talking about supporting travelling missionaries, he cites something Jesus commanded on the topic. And it is perfectly clear in all of these cases that Paul expects his readers to know what he is talking about already. The reason he can mention these things so fleetingly is that the substance of them is fully known to his readers, the early Christians.

Paul's seemingly slender evidence turns out to be highly

significant, for it indicates that what is mentioned *in brief* in his letters must already have been talked about *in detail* when Paul first taught his converts face to face years earlier. Akenson says...

> *...that Saul did indeed know the life of the historical Yeshua; that he had a full awareness of the miracles stories, sayings, and of various folk-beliefs about Yeshua, most of which are now forever lost; that he taught the most important stories and sayings to his own followers.*[20]

Akenson is no defender of the Christian faith. He is sceptical about many things, including whether Paul agreed with Jesus on certain matters of life and doctrine (a more controversial part of Akenson's argument).

RICH DETAIL

So, what information can we glean about Jesus from Paul's letters alone? Donald Akenson lists about 15 historical details unassumingly tucked away in these earliest sources. Other scholars detect more than 20 pieces of historical data. The following list is not comprehensive:

- The name Jesus (1 Thessalonians 1 v 1 and in just about every other paragraph of his letters).
- Jesus was born of a Jewish woman and was therefore a Jew himself (Galatians 4 v 4), from the lineage of king David (Romans 1 v 3).
- Jesus' earthly mission focused almost exclusively on the Jewish people (Romans 15 v 8).

---

20 Donald Akenson *Saint Saul: A Skeleton Key to the Historical Jesus*, (Oxford University Press, 2000), p 173.

- Jesus had several brothers (1 Corinthians 9 v 5), one of whom was named James (Galatians 1 v 19).

- Jesus appointed a special group of Twelve apostles (1 Corinthians 15 v 5) two of whom acquired special status as "pillars", Cephas/Peter and John (Galatians 2 v 9).

- Jesus was called "the Christ/Messiah" (Romans 9 v 3-5).

- Jesus granted his missionaries the right to material support from fellow believers (1 Corinthians 9 v 14).

- Jesus taught on marriage (1 Corinthians 7 v 10), summarized his "law" in terms of compassion (Galatians 6 v 2), and declared that he would return in glory (1 Thessalonians 4 v 15).

- Jesus had a special last meal with his disciples, which involved bread and wine (1 Corinthians 11 v 23-25).

- Jesus was betrayed by one of his companions on the night of the Last Supper (1 Corinthians 11 v 23).

- Jesus was executed by crucifixion (Philippians 2 v 8).

- Jesus was buried in a tomb (1 Corinthians 15 v 4) rather than left to the elements (as convicted criminals frequently were).

- Jesus was raised to life (Romans 1 v 4).

- The risen Jesus appeared to many, including Peter/Cephas, his brother James and Paul himself (1 Corinthians 15 v 5-6).

Paul's letters were not intended to *inform* readers about the life of Jesus (as the Gospels clearly were). Paul just *assumes* that his readers know this stuff already. And *that* is the significant historical point: the narrative of Jesus was so widely known among Christians by the middle of the first century that Paul could allude to all of the details listed above and be confident that his readers knew exactly what he was talking about. The passing nature of these references and the occasional nature of Paul's letters means that, in reality, this list must be the tip of the iceberg of what Paul and his converts knew about Jesus. Paul's letters are a very different kind of literature from that of the Gospels, but the same historical life lies behind both.

PAUL AND ORAL TRADITION

Paul's letters take us to the middle of the first century, approximately 20 years after Jesus. That is a relatively small time gap by ancient standards (remember, Tacitus wrote his account of Tiberias almost 80 years after the emperor died). Yet one passage from Paul (which I will quote below) takes us much closer, to within just a few of years of the crucifixion.

In his letter to the Corinthians, penned about AD 55/56, Paul, stops to remind his readers of the core message he preached to them when he was in Corinth five years earlier (AD 50). He does this in the common ancient style of a pithy, memorable summary—what you might call a "creed"—which the Corinthians learned by heart when Paul was with them. Primary schools in Paul's day used such mnemonic summaries to learn the basics of, for example, speech writing. And even the philosophical schools for adults, such as the School of the Epicureans, employed memorable summaries to lock into the minds of students the central arguments of Epicurus.[21]

Here is one of the striking differences between the world

---

21 I am in the process of writing a book—a very different kind of book—about the use of memory in ancient education; I won't bore you with further details.

we inhabit and the one the first Christians inhabited. Today, we hardly use our memories at all. Why would we? We've got our phones and Google. But in ancient times the memory was regarded as a foundational intellectual organ, almost on a par with reasoning.

Perhaps the only relic of the once omnipresent act of disciplined *remembering* is the way many of us can recall the song lyrics of our favourite bands. To this day, I can sing along to virtually all the songs of the seven U2 albums from *Boy* (1982) to *Rattle and Hum* (1988). That's 78 songs. At approximately 150 words per song, I probably know by heart approximately 11,700 words of U2. Coincidentally, that's roughly 40 pages of this book, or about the length of the entire Gospel of Mark.

Jewish rabbis in the ancient world, just like philosophical teachers, often made their disciples learn key statements by rote. This was a way of safeguarding the most important ideas. Here's an example. Using the well-known jargon of oral tradition, the first-century Jewish writer Josephus tells us that…

> …*the Pharisees had passed on [paradidōmi)]to the people certain regulations handed down by former generations and not recorded in the Laws of Moses.*
>
> ANTIQUITIES 13.297

The key terminology here—which was also used in philosophical schools—was "to pass on" (*paradidōmi*) and "to receive" (*paralambanō*): one was the duty of the teacher, the other the duty of the student. Paul himself was a former Pharisee, and he employed the same practice to good effect among his non-Jewish hearers. What is fascinating in the paragraph quoted below is that Paul admits that *he* is not the source of the oral summary or creed that he passed on to his converts. Just as the Corinthians "received" it from Paul when he was with them in AD 50, so Paul "received" it from others when he first learnt about Christ. Given that we know when Paul became a disciple, this statement must date to the early 30s. Here it is (with the "creed" in bold):

Now, brothers and sisters, I want to remind you of the gospel I preached to you, which you received and on which you have taken your stand. By this gospel you are saved, if you hold firmly to the word I preached to you. Otherwise, you have believed in vain. For what I received [paralambanō] I passed on [paradidōmi] to you as of first importance:

that Christ died for our sins
   according to the Scriptures,
that he was buried,
that he was raised on the third day
   according to the Scriptures,
and that he appeared to Cephas,
and then to the Twelve.

1 CORINTHIANS 15 v 1-5, *emphasis mine*

Scholars debate exactly when Paul "received" this pithy creed. Some date it to the year of his conversion in AD 31/32 (in Damascus), and others to AD 33/34 when Paul spent fifteen days in Jerusalem in conversation with the apostle Peter and Jesus' brother James (Galatians 1 v 18-20).

Whichever date we accept, James Dunn of the University of Durham, UK speaks for many when he says, "This tradition (1 Corinthians 15 v 3-5), we can be entirely confident, was formulated as tradition within months of Jesus' death."[22] This is as close to the events themselves as a historian could hope for.

---

22 James Dunn, *Jesus Remembered* (Eerdmans, 2003), p 855.

The significance of this creed is obvious. It establishes beyond reasonable doubt that at least six elements of the narrative of Jesus arose *immediately* after his death and could not be part of some developing legend. Already by AD 35 at the latest...

- Jesus' status as Christ or Messiah,
- his death for sins,
- his burial in a tomb,
- his resurrection after three days,
- his multiple appearances, and,
- his appointment of twelve apostles

...were all sufficiently well known to have become part of a formal summary of Christianity which was passed onto converts far and wide. This proves—in the historian's sense of the word "prove"—that what was later written down in detail in the Gospels, and hinted at throughout Paul's letters, was already being proclaimed by missionaries and committed to memory by disciples within months of the events themselves.

In A Nutshell

The letters of Paul, a former persecutor of Christians, are our earliest sources for the historical Jesus, dating to within 20 years of the events themselves. Their significance lies not only in their early dates but in the way they show—by their multiple passing mentions of things Jesus said and did—that a great deal of information about Jesus was already known by Paul's readers *before* he wrote to them, and long before the Gospels were composed. And one passage in Paul's epistles (1 Corinthians 15 v 1-5) provides the professional historian with confidence that the *core* of the story was fixed—in creed and in memory—within the first months and years after the events themselves.

Readings

A sample of Paul's letters

[To Rome]: Love must be sincere. Hate what is evil; cling to what is good. Be devoted to one another in love. Honour one another above yourselves. Never be lacking in zeal, but keep your spiritual fervour, serving the Lord. Be joyful in hope, patient in affliction, faithful in prayer. Share with the Lord's people who are in need. Practise hospitality. Bless those who persecute you; bless and do not curse. Rejoice with those who rejoice; mourn with those who mourn. Live in harmony with one another. Do not be proud, but be willing to associate with people of low position. Do not be conceited. Do not repay anyone evil for evil. Be careful to do what is right in the eyes of everyone. If it is possible, as far as it depends on you, live at peace with everyone.

ROMANS 12 v 9-18

[To Thessalonica] Now about your love for one another we do not need to write to you, for you yourselves have been taught by God to love each other. And in fact, you do love all of God's family throughout Macedonia. Yet we urge you, brothers and sisters, to do so more and more, and to make it your ambition to lead a quiet life: You should mind your own business and work with your hands, just as we told you, so that your daily life may win the respect of outsiders and so that you will not be dependent on anybody.   1 Thessalonians 4 v 9-12

[To Philippi] Do nothing out of selfish ambition or vain conceit. Rather, in humility value others above yourselves, not looking to your own interests but each of you to the interests of the others.

In your relationships with one another, have the same mindset as Christ Jesus: who, being in very nature God, did not consider equality with God something to be used to his own advantage; rather, he made himself nothing by taking the very nature of a servant, being made in human likeness. And being found in appearance as a man, he humbled himself by becoming obedient to death—even death on a cross! Therefore God exalted him to the highest place and gave him the name that is above every name, that at the name of Jesus every knee should bow, in heaven and on earth and under the earth, and every tongue acknowledge that Jesus Christ is Lord, to the glory of God the Father.

Philippians 2 v 3-11

The first four of 40 pithy summaries of the teaching of Epicurus, which *all* Epicurean students were meant to memorise

1. A blessed and eternal being has no trouble himself and brings no trouble upon any other being; hence he is exempt from movements of anger and partiality, for every such movement implies weakness.

2. Death is nothing to us; for the body, when it has been resolved into its elements, has no feeling, and that which has no feeling is nothing to us.

3. The magnitude of pleasure reaches its limit in the removal of all pain. When pleasure is present, so long as it is uninterrupted, there is no pain either of body or of mind or of both together.

4. Continuous pain does not last long in the flesh; on the contrary, pain, if extreme, is present a very short time, and even that degree of pain which barely outweighs pleasure in the flesh does not last for many days together. Illnesses of long duration even permit of an excess of pleasure over pain in the flesh.

Diogenes Laertius, EPICURUS 10.139-40

Digging stuff up

Archaeology was once about digging up "proof" for the Bible, and discovering ancient treasures. This is no longer the case. Archaeology today is a highly regulated research discipline that seeks to uncover the *material* remains of the ancient world—buildings, coins, inscriptions, domestic artefacts and so on—in order to bring these into conversation with the literary evidence of the period, in an effort to clarify the geopolitics, economics and ordinary life in the society under investigation.

As you are reading these words, scores of digs are being conducted throughout Galilee and Judaea—in the modern state of Israel—which are yielding fascinating results for the study of our period generally, and Jesus in particular. I want to present a few *interesting if trivial* examples of archaeological discoveries in Israel, and then one *seemingly mundane but highly significant* example that resolves a problem which scholars have long pondered concerning the Gospels.

A POOL

In passing, the Gospel of John mentions a public pool in Jerusalem featuring five colonnades or rows of columns. Jesus is said to have healed someone there:

> *Now there is in Jerusalem near the Sheep Gate a pool, which in Aramaic is called Bethesda and which is surrounded by five covered colonnades. Here a great number of disabled people used to lie—the blind, the lame, the paralysed. One who was there had been an invalid for thirty-eight years. When Jesus saw him lying there and learned that he had been in this condition for a long time, he asked him, "Do you want to get well?" "Sir," the invalid replied, "I have no one to help me into the pool when the water is stirred. While I am trying to get in, someone else goes down ahead of me." Then Jesus said to him, "Get up! Pick up your mat and walk." At once the man was cured; he picked up his mat and walked.* JOHN 5 v 1-8

Archaeological digs throughout Jerusalem failed to discover a pool near where (we thought) the Sheep Gate was—certainly not a pool with the highly unusual "five covered colonnades". Some scholars began proposing that such geographical details in John's Gospel were either fictitious or symbolic. However, a series of archaeological investigations in 1957-1962 uncovered a pool in the very area described by John; and, yes, there were five colonnades, one on each of the four edges of the pool and one across the middle dividing the pool from west to east.[23]

Commentators who had doubted such geographical de-

23 Urban C. von Wahlde, "Archaeology and John's Gospel" (p 523-586) in *Jesus and Archaeology*, edited by James H. Charlesworth. (Eerdmans, 2006), p 566.

tails were making the fundamental mistake of supposing that absence of corroborating evidence implied evidence of absence. Scholars are usually more wary of such assumptions. History is too random and fragmentary for us to make firm judgements on the basis of limited evidence about what possibly did *not* exist.

AN INSCRIPTION

In chapter 7 I discussed an inscription mentioning Pontius Pilate. It dedicates a building in Caesarea Maritima on the coast of Israel (where it was discovered) to the honour of Emperor Tiberius. Pilate, who mostly lived in this coastal town, not Jerusalem, managed to slip his own name into one of the four Latin lines:

Caesareans' Tiberium
Pontius Pilate
Prefect of Judaea
dedicates

The inscription confirms Pontius Pilate's precise administrative title. I mentioned earlier that the great Roman chronicler Tacitus in his statement about Jesus' execution mistakenly calls Pilate a "procurator", another kind of governor of the ancient world. But this title was not given to such Roman officials in this region until a decade after Pilate. Pilate's real title was "Prefect of Judaea".

While Tacitus gets it wrong, the Gospels rightly call Pilate *hegemon,* a general Greek term for *governor* or *prefect*.

SOME BONES

My final interesting archaeological discovery concerns crucifixion. To date, just one piece of physical evidence of this barbarous method of execution has been found. Numerous documents from the ancient world mention crucifixion, but since victims of crucifixion were normally thrown into shallow graves or left to the elements, our chances of uncovering archaeological remains of the practice were always low.

It is on this basis that a few scholars, as well as many popular sceptics, have suggested that Jesus would not have been "buried" in a tomb, as the New Testament writers claim. French philosopher and atheist Michel Onfray declares:

> *But let us concede that he was put on the cross. In that case, like all other such victims, he would have been left hanging there, at the mercy of wild beasts ... Then the remains were thrown into a common grave. In any case, there was no question of bodies being laid to rest in tombs. Fabrications.*[24]

It is strong stuff, but it is entirely mistaken.

In 1968 Israeli archaeologists discovered a tomb just north of Jerusalem containing some Jewish burial boxes (ossuaries). One ossuary was inscribed "Jehohanan and Jehohanan ben Jehohanan", meaning that the box contained the bones of a father and his son of the same name. Analysis of the bones revealed a male right heel bone which had been pierced through with an iron nail. This man was clearly a victim of crucifixion. The nail, which was 11.5cm long, was badly bent and so had never been removed from the foot. A plaque of wood from an olive tree was still attached. It was a remarkable find, and confirms that some crucifixion victims certainly did receive a proper burial.[25]

---

24 Michael Onfray, *Atheist Manifesto*. (Arcade Publishing, 2005), p 128.
25 The definitive report of the find is in J. Zias and E. Sekeles, "The Crucified Man from Giv'at ha-Mivtar: A Reappraisal," *Israel Exploration Journal* 35 (1985), p 22-27.

A GALILEAN STORY IN THE GREEK LANGUAGE?

I want to offer a more mundane (perhaps boring) *but highly significant* example of the way archaeology assists the contemporary study of Jesus. It has long been observed that the Gospels tell a very *Jewish* story, and yet the language in which this story is told is not Aramaic or Hebrew—the languages of Jews of this time and place—but Greek, the language of the wider Graeco-Roman world. This would mean either...

a. that there is a large cultural gap between the originally Jewish Jesus and the Greek telling of his story, or
b. that the Christian movement was more Greek from the beginning and all that Jewish stuff in the Gospels is a kind of fictional embellishment.

This may seem like an arcane line of inquiry, but such a basic cultural discrepancy between a figure and the writings about him would be more significant to the historian than any particular error of fact in the accounts. But, again, the archaeology has proven helpful in clarifying the situation.

There is no doubt that the Gospels tell a very Jewish story. Archaeology now confirms this broad picture. Work throughout Lower Galilee (where Jesus was from) has uncovered the telltale signs of Jewish culture:

- The remains of synagogues, clearly dating to the first century, in Capernaum, Gamla, and recently in Magdala.
- Bowls made from limestone, which Jews, in particular, believed maintained the purity of food.
- Ritual baths called *mikva'ot,* which were a special concern of Jewish priests and Pharisees.
- Remains of distinctly Jewish burial practices.

- An absence of pig bones in the rubbish dumps on the edge of these towns, suggesting that the local population avoided pork in obedience to peculiarly Jewish customs (everyone else in the ancient world loved pork).

There is now little doubt that the region of Jesus' public ministry was piously Jewish, just as the Gospels suggest. The archaeological evidence coheres perfectly with the literary evidence. The Jewishness of Galilee in the first century is now regarded as confirmed.

WHY IN GREEK?

But why is a Jewish story written not in Aramaic or Hebrew but in the Greek of the *pagan* world? Might this not suggest that there is a significant cultural "distance" between Jesus himself and the Gospels written about him? Once again, archaeology has helped answer the question.

Beginning with the great Tübingen University scholar Martin Hengel, we have slowly come to appreciate just how widely used the Greek language was in Jewish Israel in the first century. From the plethora of Greek inscriptions and papyrus fragments that have been discovered in the area, it is estimated that as much as 15% of the population of Jerusalem spoke Greek as a first language.[26]

More recently, we have learned there was a significant Greek-speaking synagogue right next to the temple in Jerusalem. A large synagogue inscription of ten lines was found dumped in a cistern just south of the Temple Mount. It reads (in part):

---

26 Martin Hengel, *Judaism and Hellenism* (Fortress Press, 1991).

> *Theodotos son of Vettenos, priest and synagogue leader*
> *[archisynagogos], son of a synagogue leader, grandson of*
> *a synagogue leader, built the synagogue for the reading*
> *of the Law and teaching of the Commandments, and*
> *the guest-house and the other rooms and water installa-*
> *tions for the lodging of those who are in need.*

The find is highly significant. It shows that Greek was so prevalent in Jesus' day that the holy city itself was catering for Jews whose preferred language was Greek.

Then there are the burial inscriptions in Judaea and Galilee which also reveal the wide use of the Greek language among Jews. Jewish burial techniques involved placing your loved one in a tomb, returning a year later, and then carefully placing the bones of the deceased in a limestone box (ossuary) which was then stored in a niche in the wall to make room for other family members.

Many of the Jewish ossuaries of the period have inscriptions, and it is clear that it was not uncommon for individuals to have both a Jewish name and a Greek name. One ossuary is inscribed "Judah" and "Jason"; another has "Mara" and "Alexas"; still another has "Sara" and "Aristobula". Other ossuaries are inscribed with just one name written twice, once in Aramaic/Hebrew and then again in Greek: for example, "Shalom wife of Kunoros"; "Yehuda the beautiful", and so on.[27] What all this means is that a significant portion of the population had both Aramaic and Greek as "heart languages"— languages they literally took to the grave.

It is no longer possible with historical credibility to posit a time gap, or a cultural gap, between the Aramaic context of Jesus and the Greek context of the Gospels. Many Jews in Jesus'

---

27   See the Corpus Inscriptionum referenced on p 37 for the details.

time and place used Greek as a first or second language. This chimes with the fact that two of Jesus' Galilean disciples even went by Greek names—Andrew and Philip. Like the Jewish people named on some of the ossuary boxes, they no doubt also had Aramaic names, but the fact that we are told their Greek names suggests that their families spoke at least some Greek.

The point is significant for historical studies, even if, as I warned, it might sound a little boring. What we have in the Greek Gospels is unlikely to be a late, foreign rendition of an earlier Aramaic (and therefore different) story of Jesus. It is now clear from literary *and especially archaeological* evidence that the Aramaic stories and teachings of Jesus were probably being recast into Greek by eyewitnesses in Jerusalem within months of their first communication.

In A Nutshell

Archaeology confirms numerous incidental details of the New Testament, but its real importance lies in the way it has unearthed *deep cultural realities* of first-century Galilee and Judaea which wholly correspond to the portrait provided by the written Gospels. The news of Israel's Messiah who challenged priestly and Pharisaic authorities, proclaimed the kingdom of God, died as an atoning sacrifice, and so on, could very plausibly have been told *in Greek* from the very beginning.

Readings

Jesus' critique of his fellow Jews in Jerusalem

Then Jesus said to the crowds and to his disciples: "The teachers of the law and the Pharisees sit in Moses' seat. So you must be careful to do everything they tell you. But do not do what they do, for they do not practise what they preach. They tie up heavy, cumbersome loads and put them on other people's shoulders, but they themselves are not willing to lift a finger to move them.

"Everything they do is done for people to see: they make their phylacteries wide and the tassels on their garments long; they love the place of honour at banquets and the most important seats in the synagogues; they love to be greeted with respect in the market-places and to be called "Rabbi" by others. But you are not to be called "Rabbi", for you have one Teacher, and you are all brothers. And do not call anyone on earth "father", for you have one Father, and he is in heaven. Nor are you to be called instructors, for you have one Instructor, the Messiah. The greatest among you will be your servant. For those who exalt themselves will be humbled, and those who humble themselves will be exalted.

"Woe to you, teachers of the law and Pharisees, you hypocrites! You shut the door of the kingdom of heaven in people's faces. You yourselves do not enter, nor will you let those enter who are trying to...

"Woe to you, teachers of the law and Pharisees, you hypocrites! You give a tenth of your spices—

mint, dill and cumin. But you have neglected the more important matters of the law—justice, mercy and faithfulness." Matthew 23 v 1-23 (excerpts)

The expansion of Christianity in Jerusalem in the first year after Jesus

In those days when the number of disciples was increasing, the Hellenistic Jews among them complained against the Hebraic Jews because their widows were being overlooked in the daily distribution of food. So the Twelve gathered all the disciples together and said, "It would not be right for us to neglect the ministry of the word of God in order to wait on tables. Brothers and sisters, choose seven men from among you who are known to be full of the Spirit and wisdom. We will turn this responsibility over to them and will give our attention to prayer and the ministry of the word." This proposal pleased the whole group. They chose Stephen, a man full of faith and of the Holy Spirit; also Philip, Procorus, Nicanor, Timon, Parmenas, and Nicolas from Antioch, a convert to Judaism. They presented these men to the apostles, who prayed and laid their hands on them.

So the word of God spread. The number of disciples in Jerusalem increased rapidly, and a large number of priests became obedient to the faith.

Acts 6 v 1-7

Raised
expectations

Did Jesus rise again from the dead? It's a question that takes us to the "pointy end" of Christianity. Hanging in the balance is the intellectual credibility of Christianity, and its claimed eternal relevance.

There is no doubt that Jesus' resurrection is foundational to the whole Christian faith. If *it* lacks credibility, I can see why a reasonable person would question the whole thing. And the central offer of "eternal life" rests on this claim that one person passed through death to life. Without the resurrection, Christianity is just another social movement.

In what follows, I will focus principally on intellectual questions about the resurrection, and, in particular, on whether we can say anything meaningful about it from the *historical* point of view. Then, in the epilogue I will offer a thought or two about the personal (and potentially eternal) significance of it all. But, first, I need to offer a few introductory thoughts.

MIRACLES AND THE HISTORIAN

Reports of miracles in ancient (or modern) sources present a problem for the historian. The task of analysis can be going along just fine: the texts are dated, the background material is assessed, and slowly but surely a plausible picture of a teacher like Jesus emerges from the evidence. But then, just as everything seems to be working well, we come across claims in our sources that make us wonder if we've been analysing a fairytale or legend—portents in the night sky, healings of the blind and lame, and to cap it all, a resurrection.

This is not just a problem of the Gospels. We have healing stories in some of our best material about the emperors. For example, Tacitus tells us that Vespasian—while in Alexandria on route to Rome, where he would be become emperor in AD 69—healed a man who was blind and another who had a withered hand:

> *Vespasian, believing that his good fortune was capable of anything and that nothing was any longer incredible, with a smiling countenance, and amid intense excitement on the part of the bystanders, did as he was asked to do. The hand was instantly restored to use, and the day again shone for the blind man. Both facts are told by eye-witnesses even now when falsehood brings no reward.* HISTORIES 4.81

A story like this in no way undermines the broader narrative that Tacitus tells us about the rise and reign of Vespasian. Historians may or may not personally believe that miracles are possible, but they certainly understand that ancient people thought miracles were possible, and stories like these can be genuine reports which have a simple natural explanation. In the case of Vespasian, one plausible scholarly conjecture is that this was a kind of "photo opportunity" created by Vespasian and his PR team as they made their way to Rome to claim imperial power. As confronting as miracle stories might be to modern readers, they do not undermine the general credibility of our historical sources.

I have not said much in this book about Jesus as a healer. But the firm scholarly judgement today is, as Paula Fredriksen of Boston University states that, "Jesus probably did perform deeds that contemporaries viewed as miracles". Professor Fredriksen makes clear that she does not personally believe "that God occasionally suspends the operation of what Hume [that's the Scottish atheist philosopher David Hume] called 'natural law'", but she nonetheless acknowledges that the evidence is good enough for us to conclude that Jesus performed deeds that *others* regarded as miracles, whatever the explanation.

This conclusion is shared by virtually everyone writing on the historical Jesus today. And it helps us navigate a historical approach to the resurrection. Scholars may not believe that resurrections are possible, but they can—and often do—agree that there is good evidence that Jesus' tomb was empty shortly after his death *and* that many people thought they saw him alive from the dead, whatever explains that.

MIRACLES AND PHILOSOPHY

But what can we say more broadly about miracles? The philosophical discussion about miracles has been stuck in grumpy stalemate for about 200 years, ever since David Hume's famous attempt in the 18th century to dismiss miracles by claiming that no historical testimony is sufficient to establish a miracle, unless the falsehood of the testimony is more miraculous than the reported miracle itself. It was a compelling thought, but it was soon acknowledged that his reasoning was designed to exclude testimony about miracles from the get-go, not to probe whether they are possible. Many have written on this topic.[28]

All I want to say is that both sides of the debate now generally agree that the rationality or otherwise of believing in miracles is largely determined by our *background beliefs* about the universe, not the evidence itself. If you hold one view of the universe, you are compelled to deny miracles. If you hold another view of the universe, you are free to accept miracles (under certain conditions).

If I hold that the "laws of nature" define the limits of what is possible in the universe—in other words, that no Law-giver/God exists behind the laws—then, in principle, miracles cannot be viewed as rational, and no amount of evidence could be accepted as evidence that a miracle has taken place. My background belief determines my approach to the evidence.

But there's an alternative that is equally defensible. If I hold that the "laws of nature" do not define the limits of what is possible—indeed, if I see the laws themselves as pointing to the existence of a Law-giver/God—then, since such a Law-giver could act through and beyond the natural laws, it is rational to believe in miracles, where the evidence in their favour is strong.

Readers who already think there might be a Creator—even if just a vague "Law-giver" behind the rationality of the universe—have all the intellectual scaffolding they need to accept the possibility of a resurrection. After all, they already believe that "miraculous" thresholds have been crossed in the course

---

28 See, for example, F. J. Beckwith, *David Hume's Argument Against Miracles: A Critical Analysis* (University Press of America, 1989); M. P. Levine, *Hume and the Problem of Miracles: A Solution* (Kluwer, 1989; J. Houston, *Reported Miracles: A Critique of Hume* (Cambridge University Press, 1994); J. Earman, *Hume's Abject Failure: The Argument Against Miracles* (Oxford University Press, 2000).

of deep time: inanimate molecules somehow developed into life-giving DNA, and unthinking organisms somehow developed into fully rational minds (ours) that can now comprehend the laws of nature. If these are the work of a Law-giver, it is no stretch to acknowledge that the Law-giver is able, and at liberty, to bring life out of death.

I admit, however, that for atheist readers this is nonsense. Such thresholds were not miraculously crossed; they are just the accidents of time and matter.

WHAT EVIDENCE WOULD A RESURRECTION LEAVE BEHIND?

Assuming that a resurrection is a theoretical possibility (in a universe ordered by a Creator), what kind of evidence would such an event leave in our world. The simple answer is: the *historical* kind, not the *scientific* kind.

Science deals with the repeatable, observable, and/or the mathematical. And within this sphere, science is brilliant. But obviously we cannot demand *scientific* evidence for all intellectual judgements. Otherwise, we would rule out most legal and historical knowledge. Courts of law only occasionally employ scientific evidence (DNA testing, ballistics results, and so on). Instead, most legal judgments are based on weighing and corroborating testimony.

History is like legal judgment. It is based principally on assessing testimony. If the testimony is good, we can make confident judgements. If it is bad, we are much less confident. Good testimony, as indicated earlier in the book, boils down to three things.

1. It will be *early.* That is, it will have been composed relatively close in time to the events described.
2. It will be *widespread,* which just means that it will

be corroborated (in broad terms) by more than one source.

3. Good testimony will be *credible.* Historians ask: Is the witness in a position to know the reported information? Were they around the events themselves or in contact with eyewitnesses to the events? And, does the testimony come across as sincere rather than contrived?

This last considerations may seem nebulous and subjective. But, in a similar way to judges in a courtroom, historians gain a feel for the interests and biases of their sources, and develop certain judgments about whether the ancient writer has a tendency to exaggerate or fabricate their stories.

I mentioned earlier that there is a general agreement, for example, that Arrian is a sincere witness to historical traditions about Alexander the Great. Likewise, most specialists today reckon that the Gospel-writers and the apostle Paul were not fibbing. Whatever else we may say about them, the first Christian documents seem to have been written in good faith.

The evidence for the resurrection boils down to testimony that is early, widespread, and credible. It is not the sort of testimony we would expect if the resurrection were a late-developing legend; nor if it were a fraud. It is, instead, the kind of testimony we would expect if the first Christians really did find an empty tomb and really did experience *what they took to be* sightings of Jesus alive after his death.

DOUBTING THE RESURRECTION

This distinction between scientific evidence (based on direct observation) and historical evidence (based on good testimony) explains one of the most misunderstood passages in the Bible's account of the resurrection. The Gospel of John tells how one of Jesus' disciples, Thomas, refused to believe the others when they reported to him that they had seen the risen Jesus on that first Easter morning. He responded,

> *Unless I see the nail marks in his hands and put my finger where the nails were, and put my hand into his side, I will not believe.*   JOHN 20 v 25

The original Greek language is even stronger: *ou mē pisteusō* means "Never shall I believe". This is the original "doubting Thomas". According to the Gospel, when Thomas eventually sees Jesus for himself, he receives a small rebuke for not accepting the testimony of his friends. "Blessed are those who have not seen," says Jesus, "and yet have believed." Here is the remarkable scene in full:

> *Now Thomas (also known as Didymus), one of the Twelve, was not with the disciples when Jesus came. So the other disciples told him, "We have seen the Lord!" But he said to them, "Unless I see the nail marks in his hands and put my finger where the nails were, and put my hand into his side, I will not believe." A week later his disciples were in the house again, and Thomas was with them. Though the doors were locked, Jesus came and stood among them and said, "Peace be with you!" Then he said to Thomas, "Put your finger here; see my hands. Reach out your hand and put it into my side. Stop doubting and believe." Thomas said to him, "My Lord and my God!" Then Jesus told him, "Because you have seen me, you have believed; blessed are those who have not seen and yet have believed."*
>
> JOHN 20 v 24-29

It is important to realise that Jesus is not saying, *You, Thomas, believe with evidence; but blessed are those who can bring themselves to believe in my resurrection without any evidence!* That is often how people perceive the Christian faith—as if it were about believing stuff blindly, without evidence, or even contrary to the evidence. The British atheist A.C. Grayling cited this Thomas story in a *Guardian* article, arguing that "Faith is a commitment to belief contrary to evidence and reason … [Faith] is ignoble, irresponsible and ignorant."[29]

But "faith" in the Christian tradition, as I pointed out in chapter 2, has more in common with the oldest usage of this English word: "Belief based on evidence, testimony, or authority". In this famous passage from John's Gospel, Jesus is not saying people will be blessed if they can learn to believe without any evidence. He is making the distinction between believing on the basis of *personal observation* and believing on the basis of *testimony*. Both are forms of evidence. It's just that *personal observation* is the way you determine repeatable and directly detectable things, and *testimony* is how you verify things that are, by definition, beyond your direct detection.

The fact is, virtually everything we know from history, as I have said repeatedly in this short book, comes to us via the evidence of good testimony. Blessed are those who acknowledge this.

My point is that Christ's resurrection falls into the category of a historical event. And historical events, by definition, cannot be seen or touched. They are known to us through testimony. If the testimony about the resurrection were flimsy, we could dismiss it. But the testimony is early, widespread and credible. And that's why the resurrection of

---

29 theguardian.com/commentisfree/2006/oct/19/acgrayling (accessed 4th June 2019).

Jesus remains a genuine puzzle of historical scholarship. We are not dealing with a story from J.R.R. Tolkein's fictional Middle Earth, but with a series of events—whatever the explanation—from the first-century Middle East.

So why is the resurrection of Jesus still regarded as a historical puzzle? What is the evidence that prevents even secular-minded scholars from rejecting the story outright as a mistake, fraud or a late-developing legend?

THE TOMB OF JESUS WAS VERY PROBABLY EMPTY

An empty tomb does not prove the resurrection. Any number of explanations could be offered for the disciples' discovery of Jesus' empty tomb: they went to the wrong place, some disciples stole the body, and so on. But there would need to be an empty tomb for any report about a bodily resurrection to gain traction. And the historical grounds for concluding there was an empty tomb are pretty good.

First, the tomb is mentioned in three separate New Testament sources which were not simply copied from each other: Mark 16, John 20, and 1 Corinthians 15. These texts offer *independent* testimony—they were only brought into the single volume we call the New Testament in the century following their composition. To reason historically, we have to approach these sources as different lines of testimony, all pointing in the same direction.

Second, there is good evidence that the leaders of Jerusalem in the decades following Jesus' death claimed that the disciples stole the body from the tomb to give credibility to the Christian movement (Matthew 28 v 11-15; Justin, *Dialogue with Trypho* 108). This is significant, because it tells the contemporary historian that even the critics of Christianity agreed there was an empty tomb. The dispute in those early days was not over *whether* the tomb was empty but *how* it got that way. This is a strong indication that there was, in fact, an empty tomb to argue over.

Third, and perhaps most significantly, many scholars are convinced there was an empty tomb because the accounts all agree that it was *women* who made the discovery. Women are everywhere in the crucifixion, burial, and resurrection accounts of the Gospels. And they were the first to discover the empty tomb. One of them (Mary Magdalene) was the first to see Jesus alive. "This is one of the firmest features of the tradition in all its variation," says James Dunn of Durham. While this might not seem remarkable to us all these years later, Dunn explains that "in Middle Eastern society of the time women were not regarded as reliable witnesses: a woman's testimony in court was heavily discounted."[30] The significance of the observation is obvious. If you were making up a story about a resurrection and you wanted your fellow first-century readers to believe it, you would *not* include women as the initial witnesses, unless it happened, perhaps embarrassingly, to be the case.[31] Géza Vermes, the long-standing Professor of Jewish Studies at Oxford University, concluded:

> *From these various records two reasonably convincing points merge, one positive and the other negative. First, the women belonging to the entourage of Jesus discovered an empty tomb and were definite that it was <u>the</u> tomb. Second, the rumour that the apostles stole that body is most improbable.*[32]

---

30 *Jesus Remembered*, p 832-833.
31 For an excellent treatment of this topic, see Richard Bauckham, *Gospel Women: Studies in the Named Women in the Gospels* (Eerdmans, 2002), p 268-277.
32 *Jesus the Jew: A Historian's Reading of the Gospels* (Collins, 1973), p 40.

All in all, then, it is far more likely than not that Jesus was buried in a tomb which was soon afterwards discovered to be empty.

Of course, an empty tomb can be interpreted in various ways. It is the empty tomb *in tandem* with a second detail that makes the resurrection an ongoing historical puzzle.

FROM THE BEGINNING PEOPLE CLAIMED IN GOOD FAITH TO HAVE SEEN THE RISEN JESUS

Our evidence that people—men and women—thought they saw Jesus alive in the days after his crucifixion is very strong. Hardly anyone writing on the topic today doubts it. This is because our evidence is (1) *widespread*, (2) *early*, (3) *unexpected*, and (4) *sincere*. Let me explain each of these in turn.

First, the evidence that people claimed to see Jesus is *widespread* in our sources. Virtually all of the 27 books of the New Testament—four or five of them independently of each other—refer to the witnesses. The most significant list of witnesses is found in a passage I have quoted (in part) earlier in the book. It comes from Paul's letter to the Corinthians:

> *I want to remind you of the gospel I preached to you, which you received and on which you have taken your stand.*
>
> *For what I received I passed on to you as of first importance: that Christ died for our sins according to the Scriptures, that he was buried, that he was raised on the third day according to the Scriptures, and that he appeared to Peter, and then to the Twelve.*
>
> *After that, he appeared to more than five hundred of the brothers at the same time, most of whom are still living, though some have fallen asleep. Then he appeared*

> *to James, then to all the apostles, and last of all he ap-*
> *peared to me also.*   I CORINTHIANS 15 V 1-8

Part of the reason why this passage is so important, secondly, is that it is so *early*. As I have explained already, Paul's letter to the Corinthians was composed in AD 55/56, but the middle part of this paragraph—from "that Christ died" to "and then to the Twelve"—can be dated to the 30s. It is a pithy summary of the Christian faith (a creed) which Paul himself was taught when he was first a disciple, either in AD 31/32 in Damascus, or in AD 33/34 in Jerusalem. Openly sceptical (even atheist) scholars agree that these details come from virtually immediately after the event.[33]

Because of the early date of this credal summary of Christian teaching, it is widely accepted among specialists that the claim about Jesus' resurrection cannot be an evolved *legend*, where, in the decades after Jesus (when everyone who knew him had passed away), people started to "improve" the story by having him come back to life. That just isn't possible, historically speaking. The above passage puts beyond doubt that the death, burial, resurrection, and appearances of Jesus were sufficiently well publicised by the 30s that these bits of the story were part of a summary of belief to be memorised by students of Christianity.

The evidence is also, third, *unexpected*. What I mean is that two of our witnesses were not believers when they encountered (what they thought to be) the resurrected Jesus.

As I mentioned in chapter 8, people have sometimes asked me, "If Jesus really rose again, why did he appear only to the faithful, not to those who were sceptical about him?" Well,

---

33 Gerd Lüdemann, *What Really Happened to Jesus. A Historical Approach to the Resurrection* (Westminster John Knox Press, 1995), p 14-15; Robert Funk, *The Acts of Jesus: The Search for the Authentic Deeds of Jesus* (Harper, 1998) p 466.

in two cases we know about, people who did not already believe in Jesus claimed to see him after his death. They then promptly became his followers (as you would!).

We have excellent reason to think that James the brother of Jesus was not a follower of Jesus during his lifetime (Mark 3 v 21 and John 7 v 5 are independent of each other). Yet, James quickly becomes a leader of the Christian movement, and eventually becomes a martyr for the faith. The above passage from Paul's letter to the Corinthians explains what happened: "Then Jesus appeared to James". In the case of the apostle Paul, as we saw in chapter 8, we have first-hand evidence that he was an active and violent *opponent* of Christianity (Galatians 1 v 13; Philippians 3 v 6), until he, too, encountered what he said was a sighting of the risen Jesus.

Fourth, and finally, our evidence about eyewitness encounters with the risen Jesus is plainly *sincere*. It was made in good faith. Virtually everyone working on the problem of the resurrection comes to the same conclusion, and the reason is straightforward. If the witnesses had benefited from their claims, gaining wealth, comfort, and social status, we might apply Cicero's famous dictum *cui bono* (who benefits?). But the opposite was the case.

The first witnesses to the risen Jesus experienced social estrangement, loss of property, loss of religious status (certainly in the case of a Pharisee like Paul), imprisonment, whippings and even execution. It is probably an exaggeration to say that most of the eyewitnesses and apostles died for their faith (which I sometimes hear claimed in church circles), but we do have evidence that four of the founding witnesses died for their faith in Jesus: the apostle James son of Zebedee (Acts 12:1-2); and the other James who was the brother of

Jesus (Josephus, *Jewish Antiquities* 20.200); as well as Peter and Paul (*1 Clement* 5:1-7; Eusebius *Ecclesiastical History* 2.25.5-6).

It is true that religious and political devotees commonly die for causes which they merely believe to be genuine. But the death of the witnesses to the resurrection is quite different. These were the ones who knew directly whether the "cause" they promoted was a fabrication or a real experience. No one dies for a lie they know to be a lie! "I do not regard deliberate fraud as a worthwhile explanation," writes Ed Sanders of Duke University, who admits to being agnostic about the resurrection.

> *Many of the people in these lists [of witnesses] were to spend the rest of their lives proclaiming that they had seen the risen Lord, and several of them would die for their cause.*[34]

WHERE HISTORY LEAVES US

The tomb of Jesus was very probably empty shortly after his burial, and numerous people sincerely claimed to have seen Jesus alive from the dead; this is where historical analysis leads us, and it is also where it leaves us. How we go on from these two conclusions depends not so much on the evidence but on those background beliefs I mentioned earlier and on our own preferences and experiences.

Most specialists today do not try to explain away the resurrection story. They tend to remain agnostic about it all. Ed Sanders (just quoted) speaks for many when he writes:

---

34 E.P. Sanders, *The Historical Figure of Jesus* (Penguin Books, 1993) p 280.

> *That Jesus' followers (and later Paul) had resurrection*
> *experiences is, in my judgement, a fact. What the reali-*
> *ty was that gave rise to the experiences I do not know.*[35]

This conclusion is typical of the secular study of Jesus: something very odd must have happened, but we cannot really probe what it was. Some experts, like Oxford's great Géza Vermes, go further. In his famous book on the resurrection, he analyses and then dismisses the six well-known naturalistic explanations of the evidence about the resurrection (the disciples stole the body, Jesus did not really die, and so on), only to leave readers hanging, unsure of what Vermes thought would explain the evidence for an empty tomb and the sightings of Jesus.[36]

We have the kind of historical evidence a resurrection would leave behind, and more evidence pointing in the direction of a resurrection than we could expect if the whole thing were a fraud, a mistake, or a legend. It is just a weird fact of history that in just one case we have good evidence suggesting (a) there was an empty tomb and (b) that people sincerely believed they saw the entombed man alive from the dead.

If the central claim of Christianity were not a miraculous resurrection but just some extraordinary *natural* claim, everyone would believe it—assuming we had the same degree of historical evidence which we possess for the resurrection. Suppose, for example, the central claim of Christianity was that Jesus was strongest man in the Roman Empire. He was crucified by the Romans, but—due to his remarkable fitness—he recovered in the tomb, powerfully moved the stone away from the entrance, subdued the guards with his

---

35 E.P. Sanders, *The Historical Figure of Jesus* (Penguin Books, 1993), p.280.
36 Géza Vermes, *The Resurrection of Jesus* (Penguin, 2008).

bare hands, and fled to Alexandria in northern Egypt, where he lived a long and happy life frequently outdoing Roman attempts to capture him.

This would certainly be a unique historical claim. If we had the same level of early, widespread and sincere evidence for this imaginary strongman Jesus that we have for the risen Jesus, I suspect no historian would doubt it.

This is not an argument in favour of the resurrection. But it does underline the point that the resurrection is not so much a historical problem as a philosophical and a personal one. What we do with the evidence for the resurrection involves those background beliefs about the universe, our life experience, our preferences and much more.

And so, as a minimum, I would say that the evidence for the resurrection is good enough to warrant sceptical readers picking up one of the Gospels and studying it with an open mind—and, dare I say, an open heart—attuned to the possibility that the figure described in these ancient sources is not only unique but potentially life-changing.

In A Nutshell

The New Testament testimony about the resurrection is as early and well-attested as anything else relating to Jesus. How one interprets that testimony involves much more than mere historical analysis.

Readings

The death and burial account in the Gospel of Mark

At noon, darkness came over the whole land until three in the afternoon. And at three in the afternoon Jesus cried out in a loud voice, *"Eloi, Eloi, lema sabachthani?"* (which means "My God, my God, why have you forsaken me?") When some of those standing near heard this, they said, "Listen, he's calling Elijah." Someone ran, filled a sponge with wine vinegar, put it on a staff, and offered it to Jesus to drink. "Now leave him alone. Let's see if Elijah comes to take him down," he said. With a loud cry, Jesus breathed his last. The curtain of the temple was torn in two from top to bottom. And when the centurion, who stood there in front of Jesus, saw how he died, he said, "Surely this man was the Son of God!"

Some women were watching from a distance. Among them were Mary Magdalene, Mary the mother of James the younger and of Joseph, and Salome. In Galilee these women had followed him and cared for his needs. Many other women who had come up with him to Jerusalem were also there.

It was Preparation Day (that is, the day before the Sabbath). So as evening approached, Joseph of Arimathea, a prominent member of the Council, who was himself waiting for the kingdom of God, went boldly to Pilate and asked for Jesus' body. Pilate was surprised to hear that he was already dead. Summoning the centurion, he asked him if Jesus had already died. When he learned from the centurion that it was so, he gave the body to Joseph. So Joseph bought some linen cloth, took down the body, wrapped it in the linen, and placed it in a tomb cut out of rock. Then he rolled a stone against the entrance of the tomb. Mary Magdalene and Mary the mother of Joseph saw where he was laid.

MARK 15 v 33-47

The resurrection account in the Gospel of John

Early on the first day of the week, while it was still dark, Mary Magdalene went to the tomb and saw that the stone had been removed from the entrance. So she came running to Simon Peter and the other disciple, the one Jesus loved, and said, "They have taken the Lord out of the tomb, and we don't know where they have put him!" So Peter and the other disciple started for the tomb. Both were running, but the other disciple outran Peter and reached the tomb first. He bent over and looked in at the strips of linen lying there but did not go in. Then Simon Peter came along behind him and went straight into the tomb. He saw the strips of linen lying there, as well as the cloth that had been wrapped around Jesus' head. The cloth was still lying in its place, separate from the linen. Finally the other disciple, who had reached the tomb first, also went inside. He saw and believed. (They still did not understand from Scripture that Jesus had to rise from the dead.) Then the disciples went back to where they were staying.

Now Mary stood outside the tomb crying. As she wept, she bent over to look into the tomb and saw two angels in white, seated where Jesus' body had been, one at the head and the other at the foot. They asked her, "Woman, why are you crying?" "They have taken my Lord away," she said, "and I don't know where they have put him." At this, she turned around and saw Jesus standing there, but she did not realise that it was Jesus. He asked her, "Woman, why are you crying? Who is it you are looking for?" Thinking he was the gardener, she said, "Sir, if you have carried him away, tell me where you have put him, and I will get him." Jesus said to her, "Mary." She turned toward him and cried out in Aramaic, "Rabboni!" (which means "Teacher"). Jesus said, "Do not hold on to me, for I have not yet ascended to the Father. Go instead to my brothers and tell them, 'I am ascending to my Father and your Father, to my God and your God'". Mary Magdalene went to the disciples with the news: "I have seen the Lord!" And she told them that he had said these things to her. JOHN 20 v 1-18

Epilogue:
Is Jesus History?

I will never forget a fascinating series of conversations I enjoyed ten or so years ago with a magistrate of the Court of New South Wales named James. He turned up at my church one Sunday morning, after having received a serious cancer diagnosis, and wanted to talk to someone. I happened to be there. And so began a delightful friendship with this calm-minded, intelligent gentleman of the law.

It would be easy to be cynical about a cancer patient enquiring about religion, and no doubt James's sense of physical vulnerability was a factor in his explorations. But he also said that there is nothing like the looming shadow of death to concentrate the mind and give clarity about important questions.

At first, his queries were entirely intellectual, not spiritual or emotional. We talked at length about the similarities between legal judgment (his life's work) and historical investigation (my interest). Both disciplines are based largely on the *assessment of testimony*. He openly reflected on how many life-changing decisions he had made for other people, based on his evaluation of the testimony of defendants, police and other witnesses. Rarely in a court of law are cases settled by clear "proof" (DNA evidence or fingerprints, etc.). Cases are usually settled—whether "beyond reasonable doubt" or by "a preponderance of evidence"—in large part, because of human testimony.

James read the Gospels and some of Paul's letters, and asked good questions: *When were the documents written? By whom? How "in touch" were the writers with the purported events? How do the claims of the various texts compare? How confident can we be that the testimony hasn't been tampered with? Is there any external verification?* And so on.

Armed with some basic details on all these questions, James scrutinised the Gospels, not in a piecemeal, bit-by-bit manner but in the way a historian might seek to determine the general plausibility of a source, or, as it turns out, the way a magistrate might assess the general credibility of a witness.

James came to regard the New Testament as good testimony. In particular, he judged that the claims about the resurrection of Jesus were definitely not fraudulent. In fact, he came to think that the resurrection was a real event. And it gave him some comfort and confidence as he faced his own death. His was not the full "Damascus Road experience". Right up to his death a few months later, James had questions, doubts, and even disputations about various aspects of the New Testament. He was not convinced that the Bible is "the word of God", as Christians typically see it. But he was pretty confident that the bits that recounted the life of Jesus contained believable testimony about a teacher and healer from Galilee, whose claims about himself inspired some to follow him and others to plot against him, and who eventually wound up on a Roman cross, before being declared by those closest to him to be "the risen Lord".

James' convictions (or half-convictions) about the account of Jesus were obviously motivated, consciously or unconsciously, by a range of factors. His terminal disease and his devoutly Christian wife no doubt made it desirable for him to inch towards a Christian faith. On the other hand, he was also very conscious of his reputation in the Australian legal fraternity as a cool-headed judge. He did not want to be known for doing anything rash or illogical in his dying days. All of these things, and more, played on his mind during the final weeks of his life. Both his trust and his doubts were the product of intellectual, psychological, and social factors just as Jonathan Haidt's work in *The Righteous Mind* would predict, and just as Aristotle outlined 300 years before Christ.

I saw James just a few days before he died. He was in hospital in a morphine stupor. I said, "James, it's John. Can you hear me? Would you mind if I prayed with you?" He shot his hand up through the sheets and grabbed mine. I prayed, a bumbling mess of words, thankful for his life, thankful for our friendship, thankful that James had come to believe— for the most part—that Jesus' life, death and resurrection were real and *meant something* in a moment like this. By the time I offered the *Amen*, James was back in a medicated daze. Two or three days later he was gone.

I was asked to lead James's funeral the following week. It was quite something, with the cream of Sydney's legal profession packing out the church—the same church he had visited for the first time just six months or so earlier. Speaker after speaker eulogised about James' career and character. They repeated, "He was a man of impeccable judgement". When I gave the funeral sermon I had the anxious privilege of letting his friends and colleagues know something of James's final "impeccable judgement". I was careful not to exaggerate things. I was conscious that James was reticent to be known as a deathbed convert. But I know he was keen for me to tell people that he had assessed the first-century accounts of Jesus' life, death and resurrection, and had concluded that they are "good testimony".

THE POINT OF IT ALL

And here is the twofold point of this book. First, whether or not a person embraces the Christian faith depends on far more than historical evidence (or any kind of evidence, for that matter). A book of history cannot convince people that Jesus is the Son of God, did miracles, died for our sins, rose again to guarantee eternal life, and all the rest.

Whether we accept (or reject) such things will depend on our life experiences, preferences, philosophical perspective and psychological make-up, as much as on any objective assessment of the facts. This means that anyone who wants to examine the unique claims of Christianity—which centre on the person of Jesus more than religious philosophy, morals or rituals—should do so with an honest assessment of themselves as much as the evidence.

On the other hand—and here is my second point—the best lines of historical reasoning today can and do, and probably *should*, lead fair-minded enquirers to the conclusion that the New Testament contains good testimony about the figure of Jesus. The early date of the documents compares well with other ancient sources. The sheer number of surviving manuscript copies of the texts is impressive. The style of the Gospels fits with what we know of ancient historical biography. The corroboration between Paul's letters and the Gospels (as well as between the sources within the Gospels) suggests a reasonably stable oral tradition in the 20-60 years between Jesus and the writings about him. The scraps of evidence from non-Christian writers in the century following Jesus also provide something close to corroboration of the basic facts. And, above all, the figure portrayed in the Gospels fits very plausibly into all that we know of his time and place; both the archaeological remains and the many Jewish and Graeco-Roman writings of the time make clear that the Gospels recount a genuine historical life.

We even have precisely the evidence we might expect if Jesus also rose again from the dead.

One of the leading voices in the historical assessment of the Gospels today, Jens Schröter of Humboldt-University in Berlin, describes the emerging consensus of scholars over the last 40 years:

> *In recent research one can discern a clear tendency to grant the Gospels the status of historical sources, thus to view their Jesus narratives—beyond the faith convictions that undoubtedly come to expression in them—as also relevant in historical perspective. This signifies a turning point in Jesus research to the extent that they were denied this status for quite some time. The judgement that the Gospels are ultimately unfruitful for a historical presentation of the activity of Jesus due to their kerygmatic [i.e. "preachy"] character or their literary presentation can, however, no longer convince. Instead, they are perceived as narratives that are interwoven in diverse ways with the underlying events of the life and fate of Jesus of Nazareth.* [37]

---

37   Jens Schröter, *From Jesus to the New Testament* (Baylor University Press, 2013), p 96.

Schröter's language is perhaps a little understated and academic, but his point is that the Gospels reveal to us not a myth from Middle Earth but an actual life from the first-century Middle East.

In the end, history is not usually capable of proving details. It is, however, highly effective in establishing the general plausibility of an event or person from the past. Historical analysis can lead us to the confident judgement that the New Testament provides us with *good testimony* about Jesus of Nazareth. Jesus *is* history.

And I would be thrilled if this book helps you to navigate some of the nonsense said about Jesus in the popular media today. And I would love to think it might pique your interest and spur you on to read the Gospels for yourself. So long as we do this with attentiveness to the evidence, on the one hand, and awareness of our own biases and preferences, on the other, some of us may well discover that Jesus is *not just history*.

FURTHER READING

Some readers may wish to leave their study of Jesus and the Christian faith on the previous page. Others might want to know what to read next. Below are a few of my recommendations for different kinds of people.

The Gospels

I reckon everyone once in their adult life should read the four Gospels. They are the first-century biographies of Jesus, and they have been terrifically influential in the history of the Western world (and increasingly throughout Asia and Africa). Reading the Gospels will give you a clear idea of why the figure of Jesus has been so challenging, admired and loved, as well as hated, for the last 2,000 years. Here are some suggestions on where to start:

- **Matthew** seems to have been written primarily for a Jewish audience and makes many references to the *Torah* or *Tanakh*—what Christians call the Old Testament.
- **Mark** is the shortest of the Gospels and most likely the earliest. You can read this in an hour and a half at a single sitting, but, as with the others, it is worth reading more slowly to ponder the meaning of the episodes it narrates and the words of Jesus.
- **Luke** is perhaps the most familiar form of writing for the modern, western reader, and would be my suggestion for the best place to start (even though it is also the longest).
- **John** is constructed very differently from the other three Gospels. It's the same basic historical narrative, with extended sections of Jesus' teaching. I suggest you try this one *after* the others.

Books

My favourite full-scale historical Jesus volume, and the one above all others I recommend to my students, is…

- James D.G. Dunn, *Jesus Remembered* (Eerdmans, 2003).

A really simple 120-page survey of the best of Jesus scholarship is…

- Richard Bauckham, Jesus: A Very Short Introduction (Oxford University Press, 2011).

An excellent textbook on Jesus, falling somewhere between Dunn's and Bauckham's in terms of academic level, is …

- Graham Stanton, The Gospels and Jesus (Oxford University Press, 2002).

One of my favourite recent treatments of the broader questions around the existence of God and the relevance of faith in secular times is…

- Timothy Keller, *Making Sense of God: Finding God in the Modern World* (Penguin, 2016).

A classic defence of mainstream Christian belief is…

- C.S. Lewis, *Mere Christianity* (Fount, HarperCollins, 1997).

A full-scale argument in favour of the existence of God is…

- David Bentley Hart, *The Experience of God* (Yale University Press, 2013).

My own popular-level account of Jesus' life and the core content of the Christian faith is…

- *Simply Christianity: Beyond Religion*
  (Matthias Media, 1999).

I have also written an introduction to the whole of Christian Scripture, Old and New Testaments:

- *A Doubter's Guide to the Bible* (Zondervan, 2014).

Can science explain every thing?

JOHN C. LENNOX

Can science explain everything? Many people think so. Science, and the technologies it has spawned, has delivered so much to the world: clean water; more food; better healthcare; longer life. And we live in a time of rapid scientific progress that holds enormous promise for many of the problems we face as humankind. So much so, in fact, that many see no need or use for religion and belief systems that offer us answers to the mysteries of our universe. Science has explained it, they assume. Religion is redundant.

Oxford Maths Professor and Christian believer John Lennox offers a fresh way of thinking about science and Christianity that dispels the common misconceptions about both. He reveals that not only are they *not* opposed, but they can and must work together to give us a fuller understanding of the universe and the meaning of our existence.

> *"This book is a remarkable achievement: engaging with all the big issues in just a few pages, while remaining profound, accessible, engaging and, to my mind, completely compelling."*

Vaughan Roberts
Author, speaker and pastor

thegoodbook
COMPANY

thegoodbook.co.uk | thegoodbook.com
thegoodbook.com.au | thegoodbook.co.nz | thegoodbook.co.in

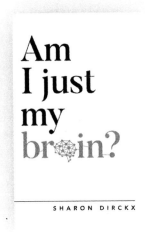

Am I just my br⬡in?

SHARON DIRCKX

Modern research is uncovering more and more detail of what our brain is and how it works. We are living, thinking creatures who carry around with us an amazing organic supercomputer in our heads. But what is the relationship between our brains and our minds—and ultimately our sense of identity as a person? Are we more than machines? Is free-will an illusion? Do we have a soul?

Brain-imaging scientist Dr Sharon Dirckx lays out the current understanding of who we are from biologists, philosophers, theologians and psychologists, and points towards a bigger picture that suggests answers to the fundamental questions of our existence. Not just "What am I?", but "Who am I?"—and "Why am I?"

"Fresh, clear, and helpful, Dirckx opens up a key part of what has been called ' the most important conversation of our time. Is freedom only a fiction? Is human dignity merely a form of "speciesism"? Are we no more than our brains? The answers to such questions affect us all, and it is vital that we all explore them."

Os Guinness
Author and speaker

thegoodbook.co.uk | thegoodbook.com
thegoodbook.com.au | thegoodbook.co.nz | thegoodbook.co.in

thegoodbook

COMPANY

Thanks for reading this book. We hope you enjoyed it, and found it helpful.

Most people want to find answers to the big questions of life: Who are we? Why are we here? How should we live? But for many valid reasons we are often unable to find the time or the right space to think positively and carefully about them.

Perhaps you have questions that you need an answer for. Perhaps you have met Christians who have seemed unsympathetic or incomprehensible. Or maybe you are someone who has grown up believing, but need help to make things a little clearer.

At The Good Book Company, we're passionate about producing materials that help people of all ages and stages understand the heart of the Christian message, which is found in the pages of the Bible.

Whoever you are, and wherever you are at when it comes to these big questions, we hope we can help. As a publisher we want to help you look at the good book that is the Bible because we're convinced that as we meet the person who stands at its centre—Jesus Christ—we find the clearest answers to our biggest questions.

Visit our website to discover the range of books, videos and other resources we produce, or visit our partner site www.christianityexplored.org for a clear explanation of who Jesus is and why he came.

Thanks again for reading,

Your friends at The Good Book Company

thegoodbook.com | thegoodbook.co.uk
thegoodbook.com.au | thegoodbook.co.nz
thegoodbook.co.in

WWW.CHRISTIANITYEXPLORED.ORG

Our partner site is a great place to explore the Christian faith, with powerful testimonies and answers to difficult questions.